First World War
and Army of Occupation
War Diary
France, Belgium and Germany

37 DIVISION
Headquarters, Branches and Services
Commander Royal Artillery
1 January 1917 - 30 May 1917

WO95/2517/1

The Naval & Military Press Ltd
www.nmarchive.com
Published in association with The National Archives

Published by

The Naval & Military Press Ltd

Unit 10 Ridgewood Industrial Park,

Uckfield, East Sussex,

TN22 5QE England

Tel: +44 (0) 1825 749494

www.naval-military-press.com

www.nmarchive.com

This diary has been reprinted in facsimile from the original. Any imperfections are inevitably reproduced and the quality may fall short of modern type and cartographic standards.

© **Crown Copyright**
Images reproduced by permission of The National Archives, London, England, 2015.

Contents

Document type	Place/Title	Date From	Date To
Heading	C.R.A. 1917 Jan-Mar 1919		
Miscellaneous	Defence Scheme 37th Divisional Artillery	18/01/1917	18/01/1917
Heading	War Diaries 37 Divn Artillery Jan 1917 Vol 18		
War Diary		01/01/1917	31/01/1917
Miscellaneous	Right Group Combined Bombardment App 68	10/01/1917	10/01/1917
Miscellaneous	Left Group Combined Bombardment App 68	10/01/1917	10/01/1917
Operation(al) Order(s)	37th Divl. Artillery Operation Order No. 41 App 69	10/01/1917	10/01/1917
Operation(al) Order(s)	Amendment to 37th Divisional Artillery Operation Order No. 41	11/01/1917	11/01/1917
Operation(al) Order(s)	37th Divl. Artillery Operation Order No. 43 App 70	17/01/1917	17/01/1917
Miscellaneous	Proposed Programme for Trench Mortars App 71	21/01/1917	21/01/1917
Miscellaneous	Reference scheme for raid.	26/01/1917	26/01/1917
Miscellaneous	Right Group	24/01/1917	24/01/1917
Operation(al) Order(s)	37th Divisional Artillery Operation Order No. 44 App 72	23/01/1917	23/01/1917
Miscellaneous	Raid.	24/01/1917	24/01/1917
Miscellaneous	Raid.	25/01/1917	25/01/1917
Miscellaneous	Positions, Arcs etc. 37th Divisional Artillery		
Miscellaneous	Medium And Heavy Trench Mortar Positions		
Miscellaneous			
Miscellaneous	Positions Arcs Of Fire Etc., 37th Div. Artillery		
Miscellaneous	XI Corps Heavy Artillery.		
Miscellaneous			
Miscellaneous	List of Positions in Area of 37th Division	06/01/1917	06/01/1917
Miscellaneous	Trench Mortars	04/01/1917	04/01/1917
Miscellaneous	Heavy Artillery Positions in 37th Div. Arty Area.	06/01/1917	06/01/1917
Miscellaneous	Appendix I to S.O.S. Orders.	06/01/1917	06/01/1917
Miscellaneous	37th Division No. G 426/28	28/12/1916	28/12/1916
Miscellaneous	37th Divisional Artillery Orders for S.O.S.		
Miscellaneous	Mutual Support 37th Divisional Artillery		
Miscellaneous	Distribution Table 5th Divisional Artillery.		
Miscellaneous	Distribution Of 56th Divisional Artillery.	30/01/1917	30/01/1917
Miscellaneous	Neuve Chapelle		
Miscellaneous	S.O.S. Rocket Signals		
Miscellaneous	Co-Operation With Heavy Artillery.		
Miscellaneous	37th Divisional Artillery Orders Appendix	06/01/1917	06/01/1917
Miscellaneous	Arrangements for R.A. Support in the event of S.O.S. Calls on 37th Division Front.		
Miscellaneous	Visual Signalling Scheme	15/01/1917	15/01/1917
Miscellaneous	O.P's on XI Corps Front.		
Map			
Miscellaneous	Directory.	17/01/1917	17/01/1917
Miscellaneous	List of Position Calls		
Miscellaneous	Right Group Left Group.		
War Diary		01/02/1917	28/02/1917
Operation(al) Order(s)	37th Divisional Artillery Operation Order No. 46 App 73	31/01/1917	31/01/1917
Miscellaneous	Table Of Reliefs.		
Operation(al) Order(s)	37th Divisional Artillery Operation Order No. 47 App 74		

Miscellaneous	Table "A"		
Miscellaneous	March Orders.	10/02/1917	10/02/1917
Operation(al) Order(s)	37th Divisional Artillery Operation Order No 48	11/02/1917	11/02/1917
Miscellaneous	37th Div. Arty. App 76	27/02/1917	27/02/1917
Miscellaneous	Programme-28th Feby.-1st March.	20/02/1917	20/02/1917
Miscellaneous	Artillery Programme, Raid by 63rd Infantry Brigade, App 75		
Miscellaneous	Trench Mortar Programme.		
Miscellaneous	Diversion on Hulloch Sector,		
Miscellaneous	Trench Mortars.	25/02/1917	25/02/1917
Miscellaneous	37th Division Q.	31/03/1917	31/03/1917
War Diary		01/03/1917	31/03/1917
Miscellaneous	RATS Programme-28th Feby.-1st March. App 77	28/02/1917	28/02/1917
Miscellaneous	Right Group. Programme-2nd March. App 78	02/03/1917	02/03/1917
Miscellaneous	Artillery Barrage During Raid on Hulluch Sector App 78	27/02/1917	27/02/1917
Miscellaneous	App 78 Reference this office no. C/119/4 dated 27.2.17.	28/02/1917	28/02/1917
Miscellaneous	Table "A"	28/02/1917	28/02/1917
Operation(al) Order(s)	37th Divisional Artillery Operation Order No. 47 app 79	27/02/1917	27/02/1917
Miscellaneous		28/02/1917	28/02/1917
Miscellaneous	Table "A"	28/02/1917	28/02/1917
Miscellaneous	Reference 37th D.A. Operation Order No. 48 para. viii. app 79	02/03/1917	02/03/1917
Miscellaneous	March Table.		
Operation(al) Order(s)	37th Divisional Artillery Operation Order No. 48 App 79	01/03/1917	01/03/1917
Operation(al) Order(s)	37th Divisional Artillery Operation Order No. 49 App 80	08/03/1917	08/03/1917
Operation(al) Order(s)	37th Divisional Artillery Operation Order No. 50 App 81	15/03/1917	15/03/1917
Operation(al) Order(s)	37th Divisional Artillery Operation Order No. 52 App 83	21/03/1917	21/03/1917
Operation(al) Order(s)	37th Divisional Artillery Operation Order No. 53 App 84	22/03/1917	22/03/1917
Heading	War Diaries March 1917 37th Divn Arty		
Miscellaneous	37th Div. "Q"	02/05/1917	02/05/1917
War Diary		09/04/1917	30/04/1917
Operation(al) Order(s)	Operation Reports. App 6		
Miscellaneous	App 7	27/04/1917	27/04/1917
Map			
Operation(al) Order(s)	37th Divisional Artillery Operation Order No. 57 App 3	17/04/1917	17/04/1917
Operation(al) Order(s)	37th Divisional Artillery Operation Order No. 54 App 1	12/04/1917	12/04/1917
Miscellaneous	App 10 S/CRA/18/91 12-4-17.	12/04/1917	12/04/1917
Operation(al) Order(s)	37th Divisional Artillery Operation Order No. 56 App 2	16/04/1917	16/04/1917
Operation(al) Order(s)	33 Div. G.S. Ins. B.1. Appendix 1	21/04/1917	21/04/1917
Miscellaneous	Dispositions of 37th D.A. App 4	21/04/1917	21/04/1917
Heading	H.Q. Ra 37 D Vol 22 May 17		
Miscellaneous	37th Division. "Q"	02/06/1917	02/06/1917
War Diary		01/05/1917	30/05/1917
Map			
Miscellaneous	Operation Reports. App M/OR		
Miscellaneous	Operation Reports.	03/05/1917	03/05/1917
Operation(al) Order(s)	37th Divisional Artillery Operation Order No. 55 App M/1	02/05/1917	02/05/1917
Operation(al) Order(s)	37th Divisional Artillery Operation Order No. 55	02/05/1917	02/05/1917
Miscellaneous	Reference 37th D.A.O.O. No. 55	02/05/1917	02/05/1917

Miscellaneous	To 37th D.A. App M/2	01/05/1917	01/05/1917
Miscellaneous	VII Corps Heavy Artillery.		
Miscellaneous	O.C. 123 Bde. R.F.A.	02/05/1917	02/05/1917
Operation(al) Order(s)	21st Divisional Artillery Operation Order No. 57 App M/3	01/05/1917	01/05/1917
Miscellaneous	Ref. 21st Div. Art. O.O. No. 57 Appendix 'A'	02/05/1917	02/05/1917

37TH DIVISION

C. R. A.

1917 JAN ~~APR 1917~~-MAR 1919

SECRET   ORIGINAL

DEFENCE SCHEME
37th DIVISIONAL ARTILLERY.

CONTENTS

1. Positions, Right Group.
2. Positions, Left Group.
3. Alternative Positions.
4. Trench Mortar Positions. and others
5 & 6. Positions, complete list of, on 37th Divisional front.
7 & 8. Positions. Heavy Artillery.
9. Positions, Right Group, 56th Divisional Artillery.
10. Positions, Left Group, 5th Divisional Artillery.
11. Mutual Support.
12, 13, 14. S.O.S., 37th Divisional Artillery.
15. Rocket Signals.
16. Visual Signalling.
17. S.O.S., Heavy Artillery.
18. Gas & Hostile bombardment.
19. Co-operation with Heavy Artillery.
20 & 21. List of O.P's.
22. Rear Lines (to follow).
23. Position Calls
24. Directory
-----o0o-----
25. R.E.

WAR DIARIES
37 DIVN ARTILLERY
JAN 1917

HQ
123 Bds
124 Bds
126 Bds
TAC
Hy + Medium T.M.

WAR DIARY or INTELLIGENCE SUMMARY

Army Form C. 2118.

January 1917

Place	Date	Hour	Summary of Events and Information	Remarks and references to Appendices
	1st		Willing's report. 37th D.A. took over line from Festubert to Neuve Chapelle both included. (SignlPost Lane on north to Pollieure on south) Relieving 34" Div.	
	2nd		A/124 position shelled by a 4.2 hy. Shooting excellent. No casualties.	
	3rd		Relieving 34" report	
	4th		" " "	
	5th		Lille – La Bassée Rd much used during evening	
	6th	2.15 pm	Working party at S.P.D.15	
	7th	12.15 pm	Railway shelled 5.20 C.9.3. a report of infantry in front line of cover trench	
	8th		Enemy found shelling of cover trench	
		9.30 am 10.30 am	about 40 77 mm and 105 mm shells fell in Neuve Chapelle. Bombardment Bois du Biez – Susceptible(?) ... was kept up on Rue d'Ouvert	

WAR DIARY or INTELLIGENCE SUMMARY

Army Form C. 2118.

(Erase heading not required.)

Instructions regarding War Diaries and Intelligence Summaries are contained in F.S. Regs., Part II. and the Staff Manual respectively. Title pages will be prepared in manuscript.

Place	Date	Hour	Summary of Events and Information	Remarks and references to Appendices
	10.		Bombardment carried o.T. of front trenches w S16 2S22 was shelled by 150 mm shells	See Appx 68
	11.	2pm D/126	Foggy and wet. Visiting trenches.	
	12.		B/24 Bdr fired on MG at S22C 56.71 obtaining 3 direct hits	
	13.		Our bombardment successfully carried out. Retaliation slight. See App 69	See App 69
	14.		Very murky day. Visiting trenches	
	15.		Very murky. Quiet day. More than 4 hrs. to span about 50 , 150 and 105 shells, some coming and fell in F11 and F12.	
	16.	12:30 & 4:30pm	Bombardment in a periods shelled on front line – S22A and S22C with 11 and 105 mm shells. Each period about 10 mins.	
	17.		B/24 retaliated on ADALBERT ALLEY S22 D 13, 34 and a dugout at S29 A 2.7. Visiting trenches.	
	18.	1.30pm 9.30am 16.30am	Bombardment carried o.T. Slight retaliation about 105 mm S20B. Enemy TM's used about 30 bombs in S1 B & C1/124 working parts. Sealed at S24 D87 shelled by C1/124 D/124	See App 70

WAR DIARY
or
INTELLIGENCE SUMMARY.
(Erase heading not required.)

Army Form C. 2118.

Place	Date	Hour	Summary of Events and Information	Remarks and references to Appendices
	19th	3pm	Hostile artillery active along left front. Short bursts throughout afternoon.	
			Enemy aeroplane flew over our front line about SSL	
		1pm	Six 105mm shells fell near C50 w30 w S25D64	
			Visiting Aircraft	
	20th	11am	Cover French worked with TM results — 2 to 2.45 pm enemy	
			shelled neighbourhood of Chateau Redoubt, damaging our	
			wire entanglements and wire. No attack followed.	
	21st	6.15 pm	Rocket & heavy firing took place on left Bde of Div on	
			our left.	
	22nd	3.30 a.m.	Our French mortars fired on and damaged enemy wire at S5-d-6.5-2.2 b. See App. 71.	
			S5 d 48-98. Enemy retaliated on the emplacements, no damage done.	
			Enemy trench mortar rampart line in M36 d S5 G1 C - S16 c - 522 a.h.	
	23rd		Nothing to report.	
	24th		Very quiet day.	
	25th			
	26th		Nothing to report. A relief was unopposed opposite the Div Group during	
			tonight, and roads and tracks were swept by MG Group.	

WAR DIARY
or
INTELLIGENCE SUMMARY.
(Erase heading not required.)

Army Form C. 2118.

Place	Date	Hour	Summary of Events and Information	Remarks and references to Appendices
	27th		Enemy trenches in vicinity of Rue Court D'Avoué and the farm itself were bombarded during the morning - see appendix 72.	App. 72.
	28th		At 3.0am raiding party of 60 men from either German trenches round Rue Court D'Avoué. One officer and eight other ranks were taken prisoners and brought back to our lines. Right Group supported the raid as per app 72.	see app 73
	29th		Gun in western form bombarded and damaged enemy wire at S.10d 6-6-6. S.10d 85-85. Retaliation was slight at S.10d 85-85, 10.40, 63.60.70-70. Otherwise a quiet day.	
	30th		Quiet day, our M's cut wire at S.10d 85-85. Retaliation slight.	
	31st		Very quiet day.	

[Stamp: HEADQUARTERS 31 JAN 1917 37th DIVISIONAL ARTILLERY]

A. Preston 2nd Lt. R.F.A.
for Bde Major
37 Div. Art.

SECRET

RIGHT GROUP COMBINED BOMBARDMENT

Date 10.1.1917.

Time	Battery	Guns or Hows.	Task.	Rate of fire.	Nature of Ammunition.
7 am onwards.	A/124 Det.Sec.	2	Enfilade front line at S 16 A 55.60 to S 16 C 78.75.		
	C/124	2	Enfilade MORA TRENCH S 16 B 18.15 to S 16 D 46.06.	2 rounds per gun per minute for 5 minutes then 1 round per gun per minute.	50% Shrapnel 50% AX.
	A/124	2	Sweep front line S 16 C 75.70 to S 16 C 92.00.		
	B/124	4	Sweep front line S 22 B 00.75 to S 22 C 88.30		
	D/123	1	DISTILLERY O.P. – S 17.	1 round per Howr. per minute.	EX
	C/15	1	PIANO HOUSE O.P. – S 24 C 4.0.	do.	
			GERMAN WIRE and FIRE TRENCHES		
7.1 to 7.21	T.M's.	3	S 22 B 05.55 to S 22 A 77.37	60 rounds.	
	T.H's.	3	S 16 A 77.32 to S 16 A 85.05.	60 rounds.	
7.2 to 7.20	C/124	Remainder	Area S 16 A 77.32 to S 16 A 93.34 to S 16 B 18.15 to S 16 A 85.05.	18-prs. 1 salvo in 2 mins. at irregular intervals.	18-pr. 25" Shrapnel.
	D/123	3			
	A/124	Remainder	Area S 22 B 05.60 to S 22 B 20.38 to S22 A 80.00 and C.T. to S 22 B 55.00	4.5" 1 round per gun per 2 minutes.	75" H.E. 4.5" EX.
	B/124	Remainder			
	C/15	3			

Time	Battery	Guns or Hows.	Task	Rate of Fire	Nature of Ammunition.
7.21	Cease firing except C/124	2	Continue to enfilade NORA TRENCH for 3 minutes.		
7.30	T.M's	6	Re-open fire, same task, etc.		
7.30 to 7.50	18-prs. & 4.5"	6	Re-open as before "Cease fire".		
7.50	All	All	Cease fire.		
8.2 to 8.22	T.M's	6	Re-open fire. Same task.		
do.	18-prs. & 4.5"	All	Re-open as before.		
8.22			Cease fire. 18-prs. watch for opportunities.		

Copies to:-
1 5th Div.Arty.
2 Right Inf.
3 Left Inf.
4 XI Corps H.A.
5 Right Group (6)
6 Left Group
7 D.O.T.M.G. (3)
8 37 Div.
9 Diary.
10 "
11 XI Corps RA

7.1.17.

sd/- H. ROUSE, Colonel,
Commanding Right Group.

App 68

LEFT GROUP COMBINED BOMBARDMENT

Date 10.1.17

S E C R E T.

Time	Battery	No: of Guns.	Task.	Rate of Fire.	Ammunition.
7.1 to 7.21 am	Z/37	3 guns	(German wire & front trenches (No:1 Gun S 11 C 01.95 - S 10 D 05.05		60 rds.
7.30 to 7.50 am	Z/37	3 guns	(No:2 Gun S 5 D 30.43 - S 5 D 22.26		60 rds.
8.2 to 8.52 am	Z/37	3 guns	(No:3 Gun S 5 B 50.20 - S 5 B 45.02		60 rds.
7.1 to 8.22am with 9 & 12 min.intervals.	V/37	1 gun	T.M.emplacements & strong points. S 11 A & S 11 B		15 rds.
7.1 - 8.22am.	B/126	1 gun	MUSKRAT O.P. S 6 A 50.40 - S 6 C 00.70 Sweep and Search.	) 1 Round per gun	
		3 guns	S 6 C 00.70 - S 5 D 30.05 do	) per minute for first) five minutes after-	200 A
practically continuous fire to keep down heads.	B/123	4 guns	S 11 A 90.60 do	) wards 1 round per	500 AX.
	A/126	2 guns	S 11 A 40.30 - S 11 C 00.90 Front line.	) gun per 2 minutes) in irregular bursts.	
		2 guns	S 10 D 95.85 - S 11 C 40.40 Enfilade.	)	
	A/123	2 guns	S 10 D 50.60 - S 10 D 70.30 Enfilade.	)	
		1 gun	S 11 C 50.30 Sweep and search Road.	)	
		1 gun			

N.B. Enfilade Sections not to take part.

Page 2.

Time	Battery	No: of Guns.	Task	Rate of firs.	Ammunition.
7.25 to 7.50 am.	D/126	1 How.	S 5 D 20.32 - S 5 D 50.25 (Comm. Trench)	⎫	
		1 How.	S 11 B 30.60 - S 11 B 65.48 (Comm. Trench)	⎬ @	60 EX
		2 Hows.	S 11 B 60.85 - S 11 B 65.82 - S 11 B50.65 (Support trench)	⎭ 1 Round per minute for first 5 minutes afterwards 1 rd.	
8.0 am to 9.0 am.	C/126	1 How.	S 5 B 8/5 - S 6 A 25.05 (Tram lines & Com.Tr.)	⎫ per how. per 2 minutes ~~in bursts~~	
		2 Hows.	S 6 C 00.85 (Group of buildings)	⎬	130 EX.
		1 How.	S 5 B 45.15 - S 5 D 70.90 (Comm.Tr.)	⎭	

Note @ Machine gun thought to be about S 5 D 4.3.

sgd. Cecil M.H.Stevens Major
Brigade Major, 37th Divl.Arty.

8.1.1917.

Copies to... XI Corps R.A.   D.O.T.M.
XI Corps H.A.   War Diary.
37th Div.   Right Inf. Bde.
56th Div.Arty.   Left Inf Bde.
Right Group
Left Group

App 69

SECRET
Copy No. RM

37th DIVL. ARTILLERY OPERATION ORDER No. 41.
Scheme of Bombardment for 13th inst.

UNIT	No. of Guns.	TIME	TARGET	Ammunition.
Z/37	2 Mortars	12 Noon to 12.20 pm	Point S 5 B 30.50 and either side of it. Also Wire in front.	50 bombs.
LEFT GROUP	2 Hows.	,,	S 5 B 80.50 to S 6 A 30.05	20 EX
,,	2 Hows.	,,	M 35 D 85.25 to M 36 C 15.00. Light Railway.	20 EX
,,	1 How.	,,	Strong Point S 11 C 60.20.	10 EX
,,	4 - 18-prs.	11.55 am to 12.20 pm.	To fire salvos at irregular intervals along Road in S 5 D.	20 A / 40 AX
Y/37	2 Mortars	12 Noon to 12.20 pm	New Trench S 16 C 95.10 to S 22 A 87.90.	50 bombs.
,,	,,	,,	New Trench S 16 B 10.05 to S 16 D 15.92.	50 bombs
RIGHT GROUP	1 How.	,,	Trench Junction S 16 A 90.25	10 EX
,,	1 How.	,,	DISTILLERY O.P. S 17 D 10.95.	10 EX
Enfilade Section A/124	2 18-prs.	,,	Enfilade Trench S 16 A 90.25 to S 16 C 95.30.	10 A / 30 AX
X/37	1 Mortar	12 Noon to 12.20 pm	M.G. in front trench at S 22 A 78.38	25 bombs
,,	,,	,,	M.G. Emplacement at S 22 A 82.31.	25 bombs
,,	,,	,,	T.M. Emplacement at S 22 A 92.31.	25 bombs
V/37	1 S.T.M.	,,	Fme COUR d'AVOUE. Also T.M. at S 22 A 92.31, but only if the shoot on COUR d'AVOUE has been satisfactorily destructive.	

UNIT	No. of Guns	TIME	TARGET	Ammunition
Enfilade Section B/124	2 18-prs.	12 Noon to 12.20 pm	Enfilade S 22 C 60.70 to S 22 B 10.45.	10 A 30 AX
B/124	4 18-prs.	,,	Enfilade Road S 28 B 20.30 to S 29 A 15.50	20 A 40 AX
C/15	2 Hows.	,,	-do-	20 EX
RIGHT GROUP	1 How.	,,	Trench Junction S 22 B 02.05O	10 EX

NOTE:- As there is no special allotment of Ammunition, sufficient for the shoot must be saved from the ordinary allowance.

Sd/- CECIL M.H. STEVENS, Major,
Bde. Major, 37th Div. Arty.

10.1.17.

Copy No. 1 XI Corps, R.A.
2 37 Division
3 XI Corps, H.A.
4 10 Squd. R.F.C.
5 111 Inf. Bde.
6 63 ,, ,,
7 112 ,, ,,
8 56 Div. Arty.
9 5 ,,
10 Right Group
11 Left Group
12 & 13 Diary.
14-15 DDTn

SECRET

Amendment to 37th Divisional Artillery Operation

Order No:41.

    Owing to two rifle mechanisms jamming, a small part of yesterday's programme for Z/37 could not be carried out.

    Further oring to an emplacement having been blown up, Z/37 will be unable to carry out the programme as laid down for the bombardment on the 13th.

    Ref.O.O.41, Please cancel programme for Z/37 and Left Group and substitute:-

Unit	No:of Guns.	Time	Target	Ammn.
Z/37	2 Mtrs.	12 noon to 12.20pm.	Wire & Front trenches S 5 D 27.43 to S 5 D 25.28	50 bombs.
D/126	1 How. 1 How. 2 Hows.	11.55 am. to 12.20 pm.	Com.Tr. S 5 D 20.32 to S 5 D 50.25) Com.Tr. S 11 B 30.60 - S 11 B 65.48) 50 EX Supp.Tr. ~~S 11 B 20.65~~ to S 11 B 65.82) to S 11 B 50.65.)	
B/126	1 Gun	do.	MUSKRAT O.P.)	
	1 Gun	do	S 6 A 50.40 to S 6 C 00.70) 20 A Sweep and search road.) 40 AX	
(Enf. Sect)	2 Guns	do	S 5 D 20.40 to S 5 D 38.00) enfilade front trench.)	
B/123	2 Guns	do	S 6 C 00.70 - S 5 D 30.05) sweep & search road.)	

                            sgd. Cecil M.H.Stevens   Major
11.1.1917.   Brigade Major,37th Divl.Artillery

        Copies to   37 Div.   63 Inf.Bde.
                       Rt.Group   D.O.T.M.
                       Left Group   File.

SECRET   app 70   Copy No. 11

37th DIVL. ARTILLERY OPERATION ORDER No. 43.

SCHEME FOR BOMBARDMENT on THURSDAY, 18th JANY. 1917.

TIME	BATTY.	No. of GUNS.	TASK.	AMMUNITION.
1.30 pm to 1.50 pm	X/37 T.M.B.	2	WIRE — S 22 C 58.70 — S 22 C 90.30.	
	,,	1	WIRE — S 22 A 72.43 — S 22 A 78.32.	
	V/37 ,,	3	S 10 D 0.3 — S 10 D 72.75.	130
	Z/37 ,,	2	S 10 D 72.75 — S 10 D 99.90.	
	V/37 H.T.M.	1	Strong Point — S 5 D 22.35.	5
To commence at 1.30 pm.	D/123 Bde.RFA 4.5" How.	—	NEi Trench S 16 D 10.20 — S 16 D 20.15.	100 EX

N O T E :-   Attention is called to aeroplane photograph No. 684.

Sd/- CECIL M.H.STEVENS Major,
Bde.Major, 37th Divl. Artillery.

17.1.17.   Copies to:-
1   XI Corps R.A.
2~~   XI Corps R.A.~~
3   37th Divn.
4   10th Squd. R.F.C.
5   5th Div. Arty.
2 & 6   Right Group
7   Left Group
8   Right Inf. Bde.
9   Left Inf. Bde.
10 A.H. Diary.
12-16 DoTM

SECRET

PROPOSED PROGRAMME for TRENCH MORTARS
21.1.17 to 27.1.17.

Date	Time	No. of Guns	TASK	Ammunition.
22nd	3 to 3.30 pm	2	Wire S 5 B 52.22 to S 5 D 48.98	60 rds.
23rd	2 to 2.30 pm	2	Wire S 10 D 72.76 to S 10 D 25.50	60 rds.
22nd.	3 p.m.	1 9.45"	T.M. Emplacements - S 22 B 12.50 and S 22 D 05.35.	10 rds.

Reference combined shoot on 25th, (Operation Order No.42). 1 Mortar of Y/37 has been taken off S 22 A 78.43 to S 22 A 78.05 and put on wire cutting at S 22 A 60.60, by request of B.G.C., 112th Infantry Brigade.

Sd/- CECIL H.H. STEVENS Major,
Bde. Major, 37th Divl. Artillery.

21.1.17.

SO/648.

Copy No......

Reference scheme for raid.

The date will be 28th inst. Zero time 3 A.M. Communication has been arranged from our front line to Group Headquarters. O.C. C/124 will report that this is complete. Code word "Robin A" or "Robin B" or "C" will be used by infantry to denote that each party A, B or C has returned. Code word "Goldfinch" will denote that all parties have returned. On this, all artillery fire will cease. Watches will be synchronised at 10.30 pm on the 27th and at 2.30 a.m. on the 28th. O.C. A/124 will be responsible for giving time to A/126 detached section, and O.C. C/124 for time to C/123 detached section.

PLEASE ACKNOWLEDGE.

R L Laver

2/Lt. R.F.A.
Adjutant, RIGHT GROUP.

26.1.17.
Distribution :-
No.1. 27th Div. Arty.
 " 2 Infantry Brigade.
 " 3 10th L.M.L.
 " 4 A/124.
 " 5 B/124.
 " 6 C/124.
 " 7 D/124.
 " 8 D/123.
 " 9 D/15.
 " 10 A/126.
 " 11 C/123.
 " 12 RIGHT GROUP.

Right Group
Left Group
D.O.T.M.

37th Div.
Right Inf. Bde.
Left Inf. Bde.
XIth Corps, R.A.
XIth Corps Heavy Arty.
10th Squadron, R.F.A.
56th Div. Arty.
5th Div. Arty.

     Will you please note that the 37th Divisional Artillery Operation Order No:42, ordering a bombardment for 25th instant is cancelled and the attached substituted.

24.1.1917.   sgd. Cecil M.H. Stevens   Major

                Brigade Major, 37th Divl. Artillery.

SECRET

37th DIVISIONAL ARTILLERY OPERATION ORDER No.41.

SCHEME OF BOMBARDMENT for 27th instant.

Hour	Battery	Guns.	TASK.	Rate of Fire.	Ammunition
11 am.	D/124	2 Hows.	Enfilade Comm.Trench S 22 C 72.45 - S 22 C 90.55	To be finished before 12 noon	60 EX
11.55 am.	A/124	2 18prs.	Cut wire at S 22 A 98.84	Deliberate.	60 A
	C/124	2 18prs.	Cut wire at S 22 A 55.55	do.	60 A
	C/124	2 18prs.	Cut wire at S 22 A 75.40	do.	60 A
12 noon	D/123 attd Rd Snp	2 Hows.	Bombard breastwork (much strengthened of late and suspected of containing M.G. emplacement) S 22 A 78.43 - S 22 A 78.05	Deliberate fire for effect.	150 EX
12 noon	D/15	2 Hows.	Bombard breastwork S 22 C 88.30 - S 22 C 85.15	do.	60 EX
12 noon	D/124	1 How.	Strong Point.Suspected M.G. or T.M.) S 22 A 89.26	do.	25 EX
12 noon	D/123 (late D/126)	1 How. 1 How.	Step along Com.Trench running S.E. from S 10 D 54.60 Strong Point S 11 C 45.30	do. do.	50 EX 50 EX
12 noon to	6" Siege.	4 Hows.	Bombard breastwork (much strengthened of late) S 22 C 52.70 - S 22 C 88.30	do	200 HE.
2.30 pm.	6" Siege.	2 Hows.	COUR D'AVOUE S 22 A 70.67 Enfilade Com. trenches - ADALBERT ALLEY from	do	100 HE.
do.	Hy. batteries	6 60prs.	S 22 C 90.51 Eastwards. EITEL ALLEY NORTH from S 22 D 30.00 Eastwards EITEL ALLEY SOUTH from S 28 B 30.80 Eastwards.	do. do. do.	50 HE 50 HE 50 HE
11.50am to 12.20pm	Sect.A/124 POINT LOGY.	2 18prs.	Search and sweep area East of breastwork between FERME du BOIS - COUR D'AVOUE.	Irregular Bursts.	60 AX
& 1.10pm to 1.40pm	Sect.C/124	2 18prs.	Search & sweep area East of the breastwork S 22 C 52.70 - S 22 C 88.30	do.	60 AX
do.	Sect B/124	2 18prs.	Search and sweep the area East of S 22 A 78.00 - S 22 A 78.45	do.	60 A.

Hour	Battery	Guns	Task	Rate of Fire	Ammunition
12.15 pm	A/123	4 18prs.	Cut lanes in wire at S 10 D 58.64 & S 10 D 48.54	Deliberate fire.	200 A.
12.5 pm	X/37 TMB	6 2" T.M's	Wire – S 22 C 52.70 to S 22 C 85.15.		300 rds.
	Y/37 TMB	1 2" T.M.	Wire – S 22 A 78.42		50 "
		1 2" T.M.	Wire – S 22 A 60.60.		50 "
	Z/37 TMB	2 2" T.M's	Wire – S 10 D 85.85 – S 10 C 95.25. (In conjunction with A/123 Bde. R.F.A.)		50 "
	V/37 TMB	1 9.45" T.M.	Strong Point – S 22 A 68.68.		As required.
NIGHT TASKS. From 6 pm	A/124 Bde.	2 18-prs.	Enfilade Comm. Trench ADALBERT ALLEY	Bursts throughout night and up to Zero plus 5.	20 AX
		2 18-prs.	Search & sweep ground either side.		40 AX
		2 18-prs.	Repeat Day programme.		30 AX
	C/124 Bde.	2 18-prs.	Enfilade wire in front of breastwork from S 22 C 52.70 to S 22 C 88.30.		70 AX
BUFF BOMBARDMENT Zero minus 4 hours for 5 mins.	B/124	2	Front line S 22 C 76.40	4 rds. per gun per minute.	10 A. 30 AX
	C/124	2	ADALBERT ALLEY S 22 C 98.56.	do.	10 A. 30 AX
	D/15	1	Front line S 22 C 68.52 to S 22 C 90.30.	2 rounds per gun) per minute.	10 A. 30 AX
	F/15	1	S 22 C 90.30		
			S 22 D 15.35.		20 EX.

N.B. Zero will be notified to all concerned direct by O.C., RIGHT GROUP.

Sd/- CECIL A.H. STEVENS, Major,
Bde. Major, 37th Divl. Artillery.

23.1.17.

Copy No. 1	XI Corps, RA.	No. 7	Right Group ✓
2	XI Corps, HA.	8	Left Group ✓
3	10 Squadron, RFC. ✓	9	D.O.T.M.
4	37th Division. ✓	10	Rt. Inf. Bde. ✓
5	5th Div. Arty.	11	Left Inf. Bde. ✓
6	56th Div. Arty.		Diary.

S E C R E T.

R A I D.

Phase	Time	Batty.	Guns.	Task	Rate of Fire.	Ammn.	Remarks
I	Zero to plus 5 minutes	A/124	2	Enfilade S 16 C 95.18 to S 22 B 00.70	4 rds.per gun per minute.	60 A	
		A/124	1	Enfilade S 22 A 78.43 to S 22 A 78.02			
		C/124	2	S 22 A 70.65	do.	10 A 30 AX	
		B/124	2	S 22 A 80.40	do.	10 A 30 AX	
		D/123	1	S 22 A 70.65	do.	20 BX	
II Until order to Cease Fire probably between plus 30 and plus 60.		A/124	2	Lift to S 16 D 12.22 to S 22 B 28.80	4 rds.per gun per min.for 2 mins.than 2 rds. per gun per min.	15 A & 45 AX per gun.	
		A/124	1	Enfilade Com.trench S 22 B.20.35 - S 22 B 35.20			
		C/124	2	Lift to S 22 B.28.80 to S 22 B 20.35			
		B/124	2	Lift to line 50 yds. East of Road S 22 B 28.80 to S 22 B 18.48.			
		D/123	1	S 22 B 20.78	2 rds.per how.per min.	50 BX	
III	zero until order to Cease Fire. (probably be -tween plus 30 & plus 60.)	A/124	2	S 16 C 95.05	4 rds.per gun per min.for 7 mins.than 2 rds.per gun per minute.	20 A & 60 AX per gun & 60 BX per How.	
		C/124	2	S 16 C 80.70			
		D/123	1	S 16 C 80.70			
		A/126	2	S 22 C 60.82			M.G.Emplacements
		D/124	2	S 22 A 62.08			
		C/123	1	S 22 A 62.08			
		D/124	1	S 22 A 92.22	2 rds.per how. per minute.	60 BX	
		D/124	1	S 22 B 12.45		120 BX	
		D/15	2	S 16 D 18.05		60 BX	
		D/124	1	S 22 C 60.78			
		C/123	1	S 22A78.22 C S 22 B 00.22			

Remarks (Phase I): Zero minus 15 .. Infantry leave our lines and push forward to about 70 yds. from German wire.

Remarks (Phase II): Zero plus 5 .... They rush forward and enter German lines.

Note:- Date and Zero time for Raid will be notified to all concerned by O.C. Right Group.

24.1.1917.

sgd. Cecil G.H.Stevens Major Bde.Major,37th Divl.Arty.

Copies to:- XI Corps R.A. — 37th Div. — Rt.Inf.Bde. — Right Group
XI Corps Hv.Arty. — 5th Div.Arty. — Left Inf.Bde. — Left Group
10 Sq.R.F.C. — 56th Div.Arty. — D.O.T.W. — Diary.

C/18/3

S E C R E T.

R A I D.

With reference to 37th Divisional Artillery Operation Order No:44. Since there have been amendments to the times, to avoid any possible confusion, the times are reprinted hereon.

Phase	Time	Batty.	Guns.	Task	Rate of Fire	Ammn.	Remarks.
I	Zero to plus 5 minutes.						
				------ NO CHANGE ------			
II	Zero plus 5 minutes until order to Cease Fire probably be -tween plus 30 & plus 60						
	Zero until order to Cease Fire. (probably be -tween plus 30 & plus 60.)						

25.1.1917.

sgd. Cecil M.H.Stevens Major
Brigade Major, 37th Div.Arty.

/ Same distribution as that of }
/ Operation Order No:44.   }

SECRET

POSITIONS, ARCS, etc. 37th DIVISIONAL ARTILLERY

Group H.Q. X 19 D 8.8.
Group zone S 16 A 8.8 to S 27 D 60.25.

RIGHT GROUP

Batty.	Batty. Position.	Position number.	Battery Zone.	Extreme Arc.	Observation Posts.	Alternative Positions	S.O.S. lines.	Wagon lines.
A/124	S 7 D 90.65 (Detached Sect. N 34 C 50.25	S 7/1 F 34/2	S 16 A 9.0 to S 22 C 9.3.	90° – 130° 150° – 182°	LADDER HOUSE S 9 C 83.15 STOCKTON LODGE S 9 D 65.52 PULP HOUSE S 9 B 10.20	X 17 D 90.25	S 16 A 65.60 S 16 A 75.70 S 22 A 90.75 S 22 C 50.70 Det'd Sect. Search front of Zone.	X 19 D 8.8 to S 27 D 60.25.
B/124	F 5 B 45.25 Det'd Sect. F 16 A 58.85	F 5/4 F 18/1	S 27 D 60.25 to S 22 C 58.78	56° – 112° 46° – 98°	BRE ERY S 20 D 30.25 CANNON HOUSE S 27 A 6.4.	X 30 C 75.20 X 30 C 75.20	S 27 D 78.55 S 28 A 64.35 S 22 C 90.30 S 22 C 60.60 Det'd Sect. S 28 A 28.03 S 28 A 78.65	X 9 C 6.6
C/124	S 1 D 38.60	S 1/3	S 16 A C.8 to S 27 D 60.25	83° – 146°	BRE ERY S 20 D 30.25 WHITE HART S 15 A 2.4 LADDER HOUSE S 9 C 83.15.	S 7 B 2.6.	S 28 A 8.9 S 22 C C.6 S 22 P 05.55 S 16 C 80.75 S 16 B 05.75 S 28 A 63.35.	C 30 E 4.5
D/124	X 30 C 53.38	X 30/2	Right Group Front.	9° – 129°	BRE ERY S 20 D 30.25	4 Guns X 17 D 9.7 2 Guns X 21 C 25.60.	S 27 D 95.58 S 28 A 75.23 S 22 D 70.95 S 22 B 00.15 S 16 C 95.70 S 16 A 90.30	X C 35.1
D/15	X 24 C 25.60		Fme. COUR D'AVOUÉ S 27 D 6.4	97° – 154°	GUN HOUSE S 20 D 15.10		S 28 A 90.05 S 22 D 11.10	X 19 C 2.8

H.Q. 37th D.A.C. C 24 C 7.7. No.1 Sect. R 19 C 6.0. No. 2 Sect. Q 23 B 4.5. "B" Echelon C 13 D 1.6.

SECRET

MEDIUM AND HEAVY TRENCH MORTAR POSITIONS

Corrected to 26th Jany. 1917.

Batty.	No. of Emplt.	Map Square	Zero line True bearing	Arc of Fire.
X/37 T.M.B.	1	S 21 B 99.72	82°	30° i.e. 15° either side of Zero line.
	2	S 21 B 99.54	102°	
	3	S 21 B 99.43	95°	
	4	S 21 B 99.22	130°	,,
	5	S 21 B 99.16	132°	,,
	6	S 21 B 99.08	130°	,,
	7	S 22 C 17.38	90°	,,
	8	S 22 C 35.15	71°	,,
	9	S 22 C 28.03	67°	,,
Y/37 T.M.B.	1	S 10 D 18.82	114°	,,
	2	S 10 C 65.33	85°	,,
	3	S 16 A 05.72	91°	,,
	4	S 16 A 05.70	92°	,,
	5	S 16 C 22.81	79°	,,
	6	S 16 C 22.78	88°	,,
Z/37 T.M.B.	1	S 5 A 78.48	115°	,,
	2	S 5 A 77.47	115°	,,
	3	S 5 C 33.40	90°	,,
	4	S 10 B 35.55	150°	,,
	5	S 10 D 45.98	85°	,,
V/37 T.M.B.	1	S 4 D 80.80	110°	50° i.e. 25° either side of Zero line.
	2	S 10 A 60.60	123°	
	3	S 10 A 85.20	118°	
	4	S 21 A 85.95	93°	,,

SECRET

ALTERNATIVE POSITIONS

GROUP & BATTY.	Alternative Position		Position No.	O.P.	Nature.
LEFT GROUP					
A/123	(M 31 B 9.6	2 guns	M 31/2	S 3 A 0.9	St. VAAST HOUSE
	(M 31 B 6.1	2 guns	M 31/1	S 3 C 5.3.	TREE.
" B/123	(M 26 C 4.9	2 guns	M 26/4	M 31 C 7.3.	CONCRETE TOWER
	(M 26 C 8.6	2 guns	M 26/3	S 2 A 7.7.	TREE.
" A/28	M 26 A 9.8	4 guns only	M 26/6	M 32 C 9.7.	TREE
				S 3 A 0.9	St. VAAST HOUSE.
A/282	(M 26 C 8.1	2 guns	M 26/7	M 26 D 5.5	TREE
	(M 32 A 4.6	2 guns	M 32/5	M 34 E 2.2	"
				M 26 C 8.1	"
D/123	M 20 D 5.4.		M 20/1	M 27 B 6.2.	TREE
				M 34 C 7.3.	CONCRETE HOUSE.
				S 9 A 8.5.	TREE.
	M 31 B 3.2			S 3 D 8.9.	LANSDOWNE HOUSE.
	(Now being made)				
RIGHT GROUP					
A/124	X 17 D 90.25		X 17/1	X 18 C 0.0.	TREE
B/124	X 30 C 5.2.		X 30/1	F 5 B 4.2.	TREE
C/124	S 7 E 2.6		S 7/2	S 7 B 6.3	TREE
D/124	X 29 D 4.9.			S 25 D 55.51	HOUSE O.P

SECRET

LEFT GROUP — POSITIONS, ARCS of FIRE, etc., 37th DIVISIONAL ARTILLERY

Group H.Q. R 29 c 1.5.
Group Zone S 16 d 7.1 to M 35 D 9.4.

Batty.	Batty. Position	Position Number	Batty. Zone	Extreme Arc	Observation Posts	Alternative Positions	S.O.S. lines	Wagon lines
A/28	M 32 C 9.7.	M 32/2	S 10 D 86.84 to S 11 B 12.23	110°-30 - 146°.20	WINTERS POST S 10 B 25.43 CIRO's		S 10 D 90.65 S 11 A 20.25 S 11 A 90.60 S 11 A 52.30 S 11 A 60.50 S 11 A 10.25	R 34 A 4.9
1 gun	X 10 A 8.6	X 18/3	-do-	74° - 123°	S 4 D 7.1 LANSDOWNE HOUSE S 3 C 8.9.			
A/282	M 26 D 5.5	M 26/2	S 5 B 45.10 to M 35 D 92.40	104° - 136°	HEATH ROBINSON M 35 C 55.15		S 5 B 45.10 S 5 B 65.30 M 35 D 70.15 M 35 D 90.35 S 5 B 00.50 S 5 B 71.85	R 9 B 2.4.
1 gun	M 23 A 25.05	M 23/1		159° - 194°				
A/123	S 1 B 4.4 S 1 B 3.3	S 1/2	S 16 A 67.10 to S 10 D 86.84	94° - 144°	FACTORY S 9 D 60.55		S 10 C 95.00 S 10 D 10.40 S 10 D 55.60 S 10 D 70.15 S 10 D 0.3 S 10 D 5.5	R 28 D 3.5
1 gun	S 19 D 20.86	S 19/1		53° - 61°	MOORHEN S 9 D 80.55			
B/123	S 2 A 67.51	S 2/1	S 11 A 92.60 to S 5 B 48.05.	80° - 120°	PORT ARTHUR S 4 D 8.2.		S 11 B 40.79 S 5 D 50.92 S 5 D 42.54 S 5 D 20.31 S 5 D 45.70 S 5 D 20.37.	X 2 A 1.1
1 gun	S 14 C 05.02	S 14/3		54° - 92°				
D/123 4 Hows.	M 32 E 4.3.	M 32/3	S 16 A 67.10 to M 35 D 92.40	101° - 160°	MOORHEN FACTORY WINTERS POST PORT ARTHUR HEATH ROBINSON		S 16 B 05.75 S 17 A 10.87 S 10 D 80.40 S 11 C 45.35 S 5 D 90.65 S 5 B 95.32.	K 2 A 3.3
1 Sect.	M 27 A 1.1	M 27/1	-do-	98° - 158°				
1 Sect. D/282	M 33 A 9.5.		-do-	100° - 170°			S 11 B 35.05 S 11 B 65.40	

H.Q. 37th D.A.C. C 24 C 7.7.   No. 1 Sect. R 19 C 6.9.   No. 2 Sect. C 22 B 4.5.   "B" Echelon C 12 D 1.6.

SECRET

XI CORPS HEAVY ARTILLERY.

Gun Positions, Arcs of fire, Night Lines, and Zecon Lines

UNIT	POSITION	ARCS OF FIRE.	NIGHT LINES	ZACON LINES
X H.A.Group	R 31 D 3.8	-	-	-
2nd London H.B. (1 Sect.4.7")	X 24/1 H.A. (X 24 A 1.7).	T 23 A 2.6 to G 17 A 8.5.	A 10 C 75.25 A 4 A 5.8	R 22 A 3.7.
150 Siege Bty. (1 Sect.6" Hows)	F 4/1 H.A. (F 4 C 4.7)	T 3 B 9.7 to G 6 Central	A 9 B 7.6. A 22 B 12.95.	-
9th Hvy. Bty. (2 Sects.60-prs.)	X 4/1 H.A. (X 4 D 1.9) X 4/2 H.A. (X 4 D 2.4)	N 21 D 2.2 to B 13 C 7.3.	S 16 B 6.0 (1 Sect.) M 36 D 5.6. S 6 A 50.05.	X 3 D 1.1
9th Hvy. Bty. (1 Sect. 60-prs.)	R 36/1 H.A. (R 36 A 3.1)	T 16 D 3.7 to A 28 A 2.8.	Reserved for C.B.work.	X 20 D 9.5
204 Siege Bty.(1 Sect.6" Hows)	X 15/1 H.A. (X 15 B 3.7)	N 19 A 5.8 to G 4 B 3.4.	A 3 B 7.5. A 10 A 15.75.	-
204 Siege Bty.(1 Sect.6" Hows)	X 11/1 H.A. (X 11 B 95.95)	No.3. N 9 C 5.9 - B 14 C 9.6 No.4. N 9 C 5.9 - B 19 C 5.1	B 5 B95.38 B 11 A 95.60	-
2nd London H.B. (1 Sect.4.7")	M 14/1 H.A. (M 14 A 3.0)	N 16 C 5.7 to T 21 D 0.0	No.1. M 30 D 85.70 No.2. N 31 A 05.30.	R 22 A 3.7
150 Siege Bty. (1 Sect.6" Hows)	M 20/3 H.A. (M 20 C 8.1)	T 28 A 0.0 to N 6 Central	M 19 C 3.2 S 5 D 70.15	-

Names	Coordinates	No. of Gun Emplacements.	Remarks.
M 23/1	M 23 A 2.8	2	Outside Div. Area.
S 3/2	S 3 B 1.8	6	Wire-cutting
S 3/3	S 3 B 8.9	6	,,
M 32/5	M 32 A 4.6	4	Too dilapidated at present to be considered.

4.5" Howitzers.

Names	Coordinates	No. of Gun Emplacements.	Remarks.
X 30/2	X 30 C $4\frac{1}{2}$.3	4	Outside Div. Area.
X 18/2	X 18 A 3.1	4)	
X 17/2	X 17 D 9.7	4)	Used as alternatives.
M 20/1	M 20 D 5.4		Outside Div. Area. Not yet included in "List of Battery Positions".
X 12/1	X 12 A 6.8	4	
M 32/1	M 32 C 5.1	4	
M 32/3	M 32 B 4.3	4	
M 26/5	M 26 B 9.1	4	

Miscellaneous.

Names	Coordinates	No. of Gun Emplacements.	Remarks.
M 33/1	M 33 A 9.6	1 How.	There is a position in an outhouse for a single How. about here; There is also a dummy 18-pr. position about here.
X 24/3	X 24 C $8\frac{1}{2}$.$8\frac{1}{2}$	4 18-pr. or How.	Only consists of 2 pits as alternatives for X 24/2 (5th Divn.)

The following positions are in the Area of the
37th Division but fire over other Divisional areas.

Names	Coordinates	No. of Gun Emplacements.	Remarks.
X 24/1	X 24 A 0.1	6	Occupied by 5th Divn.
X 24/2	X 24 A $5\frac{1}{2}$.2	4	Enfilade for 5th Divn.
X 24/4	X 24 C $8\frac{1}{2}$.$8\frac{1}{2}$	4	Occupied by 5th Divn.
X 23/1	X 23 A 9.2	6	,, ,,
X 18/1	X 18 C 7.1	6	? enfilade for 5th Div.
S 14/1	S 14 C 2.6	2	Occupied by 5th Divn.
M 34/4	M 34 C 3.5	2	Occupied by 56th Divn.
M 34/5	M 34 C 4.$9\frac{1}{2}$	1	,, ,,

List of POSITIONS in Area of 37th DIVISION

Also some positions outside 37th Div. area, but firing on their Zone.

18-prs.   6.1.17.

Names	Coordinates	No. of Gun Emplacements.	Remarks.
F 11/1	F 11 D 8.1	5	Outside Div. Area.
F 5/4	F 5 B 4½.2½	6	,,
A 7/2	A 7 B 9½.20	2	,, Properly wire-cutting position for 5th Div. Area, but might be useful as alternative for F 11/1 if required.
X 30/1	X 30 C 5.2	6	Outisde Div. Area.
X 17/1	X 17 D 9.2½	6	
S 7/1	S 7 D 8.7½	6	
M 34/3	M 34 C 5.4	2	? alternative for this on N.E. side of road about M 34 C 6.7.
M 34/2	M 34 C 6.2	2	
F 12/1	F 12 C 5.3	2	
S 13/1	S 13 D 4.5	4	
S 14/2	S 14 A 5½.9	4	
S 7/2	S 7 B 2.6	6	
S 1/4	S 1 D 4.9	6	
M 32/2	M 32 C 9.7	4	
X 18/3	X 18 A 8.6	2	
S 19/1	S 19 B 2.2	2	
S 14/3	S 14 C 8.8	2	
S 2/1	S 2 A 5.5	4	
S 1/2	S 1 B 4.4	4	
S 1/3	S 1 B 2.2	4	
S 3/1	S 3 C 6.7	1	Wire-cutting.
M 31/1	M 31 B 5.4	4	
M 31/2	M 31 B 9.6	4	
M 27/1	M 27 A 1.1	4	
M 26/1	M 26 C 8.1	4	
M 26/2	M 26 D 5.5	4	
M 26/3	M 26 C 8.6	4	
M 26/4	M 26 C 4.9	4	
M 26/6	M 26 A 9.8	4	Just outside Div. Area.

SECRET　　　　　　T R E N C H　　M O R T A R S.　　Defence　　C/34/2

I. POSITIONS OF MORTARS.　Six Medium mortars, two from each battery, will be kept in action, the remaining six will be in reserve at the Rest Billets. The positions completed up to the present are as follows:-

X/37	S 22 A 2.0	Y/37	S 16 C 2.8
X/37	S 22 A 4.0	Y/37	S 16 A 05.70
X/37	S 22 A 7.0		
Z/37	S 10 D 15.80	V/37	S 4 D 8.8
Z/37	S 10 B 50.02		
Z/37	S 10 B 60.05		

It is hoped to make many more.

II. POSITIONS OF BILLETS.　Trench billets are situated as follows:-

D.O.T.M. & V/37	S 7 D 50.30
X/37	S 21 D 92.82
Y/37	S 9 D 20.80
Z/37	M 35 C 60.30

Rest Billets. All Medium Batteries. S 8 B 32.40
　　　　　　　　D.O.T.M. & V/37 ... ... as above.

III. COMMUNICATIONS.　The D.O.T.M. & V/37 billets will be connected to each Infantry Brigade and therefore through Infantry Brigade to the Artillery Group Commanders.
　　Also to Medium rest billet and thence to each Trench Billet.
　　Each Trench Billet will be connected to each Mortar in action, and to the O.P. of the nearest 18pr. battery which fires on the same front as the T.M. battery. It will also be connected with the Battalion or battalions it covers.
　　When the Trench billet is close to Battalion H.Q. runners might be used, in order to save telephones.

IV. ROUTINE SHOOTING　Daily routine work will be carried out under orders of the D.O.T.M. He will receive the Artillery Progress reports daily, and make notes of any strong points, M.G. emplacements etc. within T.M. range and which require attention.
　　He will visit the Infantry Brigadier of FERME du BOIS every Saturday morning and the Infantry Brigadier of NEUVE CHAPELLE Section every Saturday afternoon. They will bring to his notice any points that they wish bombed.
　　The D.O.T.M. will then draw up a Table of bombardments, with hours, duration etc. for the week Monday - Sunday. This table will be sent to the C.R.A.s office every Saturday evening for approval. In forwarding the reports the D.O.T.M. will say whether he requires any covering Artillery fire.
　　The schemes will then be compiled in this office and reissued to all concerned.

V HEAVY BOMBARDMENT.　For an organised and severe bombardment, extra T.M's will be allotted and the whole placed under the Artillery Group Commanders concerned who will work out the scheme in conjunction with the Infantry Brigadiers. The Group Commanders will issue their orders to T.M. batteries through the D.O.T.M. who will be temporarily placed under the Group Commander.

　　　　　　　　　　　　　　　　　　　　　　　　P.T.O.

VI. **RETALIATION.** For retaliation, Battalion Commanders will call direct to T.M. billets. Here there will be always kept a telephonist on duty. This telephonist must know the exact whereabouts of his T.M.Officer.

The T.M.Officer will open fire at once and will call on his 18pr.battery for covering fire, direct if urgent, or through the D.O.T.M. if not so.

He will report fully to the D.O.T.M. as soon as possible.

4.1.17.   sgd. Cecil M.H.Stevens Major

Bde.Major,37th Divl Artillery.

SECRET

HEAVY ARTILLERY POSITIONS

in

37th DIV. Arty. Area.

```
1.      (M 19 D 7.4              (4.60-prs.)
        (M 19 D 4.2              (2.60-prs.)

2.       M 32 B 8.2              (4.6" Hows)   under construction.
3.       M 32 C 5.3              (4.6" Hows)        - do -
4.       S  2 A 2.4              (4.6" Hows)
5.       X  6 A 9½.8             (4.6" Hows)   Under construction.
6.      (X 11 B 9½.9½            (2.6" Hows)   Occupied by 1 Sect. 6"-Hows.
        (X 11 B 1.1              (2.6" Hows)
7.       X 24 A 1.7              (4.60-prs.)   Occupied by 1 Sect. 60-prs.
8.       X 16 B 3.6              (4.60-prs.)        do.          do.
9.      (X  4 D 1.4              (4.60-prs.)   Occupied by 2 Sects. 60-prs.
        (       2.9
10.      X 15 B 3.8              (4.6" Hows)   Occupied by 1 Sect. 6" Hows.
11.     (R 24 A 9.5              (2.9.2" Hows)
        (M 19 B 2.3              (2.9.2" Hows)
12       R 24 A 6.7              (2.9.2" Hows)
13.      R 23 B 9.1              (4.8" Hows.)  Under construction.
        (R 23 D 7.9              (1.6" Mk VII)
14.     (R 23 D 2.7              (1.6" Mk VII)
        (R 23 A 1.1              (2.6" Mk VII) Under construction.
        (R 29 C 6.9              (2.9.2" Hows)
15.     (R 29 C 7.7              (2.9.2" Hows)
16.     (R 35 C 9½.9½            (2.9.2" Hows)
        (R 35 B 3.1              (2.9.2" Hows)
17.      R 36 A 3.1              (6.60-prs)    Occupied by 1 Sect. 60-prs.
```

6.1.17.

SECRET

APPENDIX I to S.O.S. ORDERS.

6th January 1917.

The Division front is divided into two SECTIONS, - NEUVE CHAPELLE to the North and FERME DU BOIS to the South. Each Section is held by one Infantry Brigade which has two battalions in the front line. In the NEUVE CHAPELLE Section each battalion is covered by two 18-pounder batteries and 1 4.5" Howitzer battery. In the FERME DU BOIS Section each battalion is covered by one 18-pounder battery and 1 4.5" Howitzer battery. In addition one 18-pounder battery fires over the whole sectional front, but is not in communication with the Infantry.

There is a direct line from each battalion Headquarters to each battery covering it.

A Liaison Officer from each Group stops at battalion headquarters at night, but not during the day. Therefore each Battalion has with it 1 Artillery Officer and 2 Artillery telephonists throughout the night.

Observation Posts are manned from daylight till dark.

The Calls for S.O.S. are as follows:-

NEUVE CHAPELLE	Left Brigade
NEUVE CHAPELLE RIGHT	Right Battn. Left Brigade.
NEUVE CHAPELLE LEFT	Left. Battn. Left Brigade.
BOIS	Right Brigade.
BOIS RIGHT	Right Battn. Right Brigade
BOIS LEFT	Left Battn. Right Brigade.

C/5374

37th Division No. G. 426/28.

```
63rd Infantry Brigade    (21 copies)
111th     "       "      (21   "   )
112th     "       "      (21   "   )
37th Div.Arty.           (16   "   )
```
----

1. With reference to 37th Division Defence Scheme, Appendix 6 - 'Orders for S.O.S.' - in order to test the communications between Infantry in the trenches and Artillery supporting them, Infantry Brigadiers will arrange to have Test messages sent from time to time.
   The message sent will be the word 'TEST' followed by the section or sub-section ordered, e.g:-

   'TEST NEUVE CHAPELLE RIGHT'

   'TEST BOIS LEFT'

   The battery or batteries covering the front named will fire one round.

2. A report of each Test carried out will be sent by the Infantry Unit through Brigade Headquarters to Divnl. H.Q. in the following form:-

----

Message sent.......................   Date...........
                ....
Hour message
sent to
Signal Office......................

Hour first round
burst on target....................
(with any remarks)
                                          Signed.................

----

3. Any unusual delay will be enquired into by those concerned at once and a report on the cause of delay forwarded with the message to Divisional H.Q.

Headquarters
28.12.16.

R. Vincent
Lieut-Colonel
General Staff, 37th Division.

SECRET

37th DIVISIONAL ARTILLERY

ORDERS for S. O. S.

1. The S.O.S. message will be sent by telephone in the following forms:-

    Code name of Battery

    S.O.S. Section or Subsectional front.

    Code name of Battalion.

2. The call will be repeated as follows:-

    (a) The Battery receiving it - to Group Headquarters.

    (b) Group Headquarters   - Other Batteries in Group.
                                   Groups on flanks.
                                   C. R. A.
                                   Infantry Brigade H.Q.

    (c) C.R.A.   - Division Head Quarters.
                                   Div. Arty. on Flanks.
                                   Corps Heavy Artillery.

3. All guns and howitzers covering the front attacked will fire the first round on their S.O.S. Lines; the second sweeping to the right, the third round to the left. The fourth round will be fired on the S.O.S. Line again and so on.
    The fire of the 18-pounder gun will be on NO MAN'S LAND when possible. The fire of the 4.5" Hows. will be on communication trenches and trench junctions.

4. The rate of fire will be as follows:-

    <u>18-prs.</u>   Three rounds gun fire, then 4 rounds per gun per minute for three minutes then two rounds per gun per minute until further information is received.

    <u>4.5" Hows.</u> Three rounds gun fire then two rounds per gun per minute for three minutes then one round per gun per minute until further information is received.

5. Flank cooperation will be given as laid down in the Mutual Support Table.

6. Should telephonic communication break down, rockets will be sent up from fixed points and runners despatched. Each battery will have a rocket table.
    The rocket signal at present is a succession of red rockets.

7. For description of how front is held, see attached Appendix I.

                                Sd/- CECIL M.H. STEVENS, Major,
                                  Bde. Major, 37th Divl. Artillery.

MUTUAL SUPPORT. 37th DIVISION and 5th DIV.

Unit Attacked.	Code Call.	By whom.	To whom	Action Taken	Remarks
Right of 56th Divn.	Co-operate LOATED GRANGE	RIGHT GRP. 56th Div. Arty.	LEFT Grp. 37th Div. Arty.	1 Section B/282 barrage front line from M 35 D 8.3. to M 36 C 32.90. 1 Section D/125 will shell trench junctions at M 36 C 16.82, M 36 C 20.35.	Batteries covering the front attacked will fire on their S.O.S. lines. Rate of fire in all cases will be as laid down for S.O.S.
Left Battn. Left Bde. 37th Div.	S.O.S. NEUVE CHAP- ELLE LEFT	LEFT GRP. 37th Div. Arty.	RIGHT Grp. 56th Div. Arty.	1 Sect. 18-pr. 56th Div. Arty. barrage front line from M 36 C 05.60 to S 5 B 82.83. 1 Sect. Hows. 56th Div. Arty. will shell trench junctions at M 36 C 20.35 and M 35 D 85.20.	
Right Bttn. Left Bde. 37th Div.	S.O.S. NEUVE CHAP- ELLE Right.	do.	Right Grp. 37th Div. Arty.	1 Sect.A/124 barrage front line from S 16 A 60.70 to S 10 D 10.10. 1 Sect. D/125 1 How. on S 11 C 05.75 and 1 How. on S 11 C 32.38.	
Left Bttn. Right Bde. 37th DIV.	S.O.S. BOIS Left.	Right Group	Left Grp. 37th Div.	1 Sect. A/123 barrage front line from S 16 A 60.75 to S 16 C 78.70. 1 Sect. D/125 Bty. will bombard trench junctions S 16 C 96.60 and S 16 D 98.55.	
Right Bttn. Right Bde. 37th Divn.	S.O.S. BOIS Right.	Right Group.	Left Group 5th Div. Arty.	1 Sect. 80th Bty. will barrage from S 27 D 55.30 to S 28 C 10.90. D/15, 1 How. on S 28 C 10.85 and 1 How. on S 28 C 30.60.	
Left Bttn. Left Bde. 5th Divn.	S.O.S. GIV. Left.	Left Grp. 5th Div. Comp.Arty.	RIGHT Grp. 37th Div. Arty.	1 Sect. B/124 will barrage from S 27 D 6.1 to A 5 B 2.5. D/125, 1 Sect. of Hows. on REDOUBT ALLY SOUTH.	

SECRET.

DISTRIBUTION TABLE 5th DIVISIONAL ARTILLERY.

Left Group .. Lt.Colonel J.Barkley, D.S.O. Headquarters .. LOISNE.

Battery	No: of Guns.	Map Location.	Normal Zone.	Alternative Position.
119th	6	F 11 D 3.4	A 9 D 9.3 to A 9 B 5.5	F 11 B 8.5
121st	6	X 24 A 55.20	A 9 D 9.5 to A 9 B 50.05	X 18 C 7.1
52nd	4 2	X 23 A 9.1 S 14 C 10.75	S 27 D 6.4 to A 9 B 4.5	-
80th	6	S 23 D 95.95	A 9 B 4.5 to A 9 D 9.3	-
D/18	4 Hows. 2 Hows.	F 5 C 1.9 X 24 C 2.6	S 27 D 6.4 to A 9 D 9.3 37th Division front.	-

DISTRIBUTION OF
56th DIVISIONAL ARTILLERY.
-o-o-o-o-o-o-o-o-o-o-o-o-o-o-o-o-

Covering the NEUVE CHAPELLE and FAUQUISSART SECTIONS.

GROUP	BATTERY	POSITION	ZONE	REMARKS
RIGHT Hdqrs. 280 Bde.RFA. O.C:- Lt.Colonel L.A.C.SOUTHAM R.F.A. M.4.c.1.2.	93rd	6 gun - M.15.b.8.5. (M.15/3)	Covering RIGHT INFANTRY BRIGADE	-
	A/280	4 gun - M.21.c.5.7. (M.21/1) 2 gun - M.12.c.6.7. (M.12/1)		Enfilade
	C/280	4 gun - M.16.b.6.0. (M.16/2) 2 gun - M.34.c.3.5. (M.34/4)		Enfilade
	C/282	4 gun - M.15.c.8.5. (M.15/2) 2 gun - M.21.a.3.0. (M.21/2)		-
	D/282 (Howr)	2 How - M.21.b.8.7. (M.21/3) 2 How - M.21.b.6.7. (M.21/4)		-
	D/280	4 How - M.15.d.2½.1½ (M.15/1)		-
LEFT Hdqrs: 281st Bde.RFA O.C: Lt.Colonel C.C.MACDOWELL, D.S.O., RFA. M.4.b.3.4.	D/280	2 How - M.10.c.5.8. (M.10/4)	Covering LEFT INFANTRY BRIGADE	Tactically under LEFT GROUP.
	A/281	6 gun - M.11.c.4.5. (M.11/2)		-
	B/281	4 gun - M.6.a.5.5. (M.6/5) 2 gun - H.34.a.6.7. (H.34/1)		Enfilade
	B/282	4 gun - M.10.d.9.2. (M.10/2) 2 gun - N.2.b.6.4. (N.2/1)		Enfilade
	D/281	2 How - M.6.a.5.9. (M.6/6) 2 How - M.5.b.6.3. (M.5/4) 2 How - M.5.b.9½.5 (M.5/5)		-
	109th	----- - L.36.c.3.2. -----		In reserve

1. 2" Trench Mortar Battery covers each Infantry Brigade and emplacements are prepared for the third Battery in each Section, and can be occupied at short notice.
V/56th, 9.45" Trench Mortar Battery, has emplacements in each Section which can be used as required. Normally, 1, 9.45" Trench Mortar will be used in action in each Section.

Hdqrs., 282nd Army Field Artillery Brigade (O.C. - Lt.Col. A.F. PRECHTEL, DSO, RFA) are out of the line at M.4.d.65.75.
O.C. 282nd A.F.A.Bde. superintends 56th Divisional Artillery School.

(30-1-1917)

Sim Post Lane | Hun Street | Bond Street | Bond Street | Rope Street | Lothian Road.

NEUVE CHAPELLE   Fme. du BOIS.

LEFT   RIGHT   LEFT   RIGHT

| LEFT Btn. | RIGHT Btn. | | LEFT Btn. | RIGHT Btn. |

LEFT Bde.   RIGHT Bde.

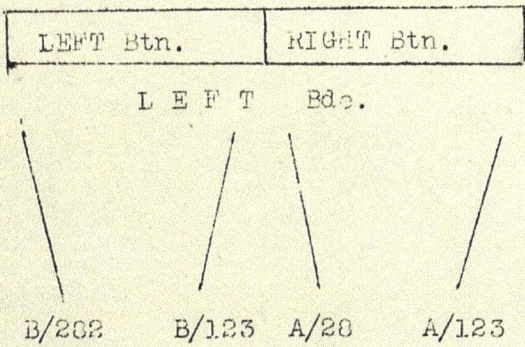

B/282   B/123   A/28   A/123

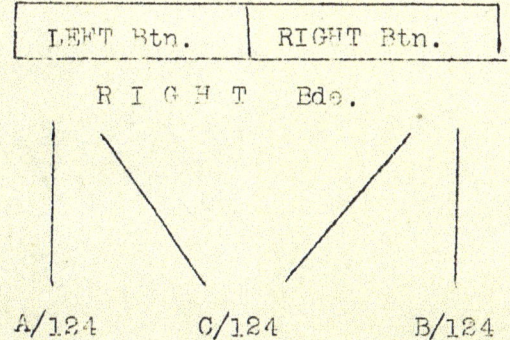

A/124   C/124   B/124

Sect. D/282   D/123   Sect. D/15   D/124

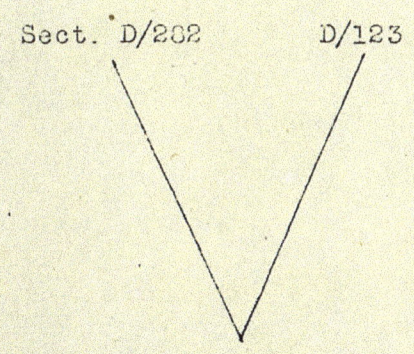

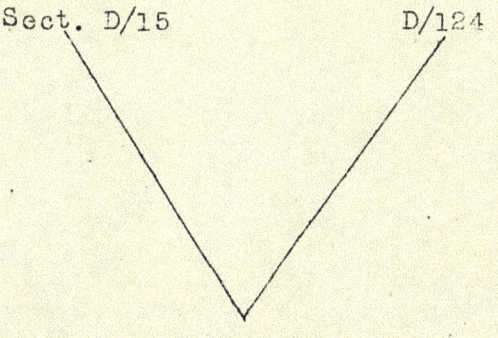

LEFT GROUP   RIGHT GROUP

H.Q. Huit Maisons R 29 C 5.8.   H.Q. Le Touret X 16 D 65.75.

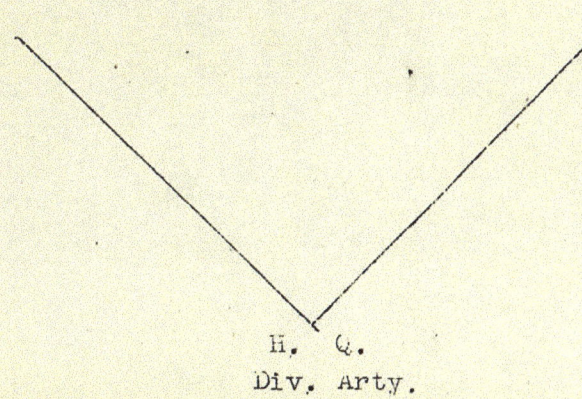

H. Q.
Div. Arty.

S. O. S.

ROCKET SIGNALS

Each Battery Position has a Rocket board. The board has a moveable pointer and an arc. The pointer cannot turn beyond two stops, which define the zone of the Battery. The usual custom is to lay the Pointer at night on the centre of the battery zone. All Batteries know the exact locality of all rocket stands in the subsections they cover. Sentries are posted at night to look out for rockets.

ROCKETS are sent up as follows:-

RIGHT GROUP	1.	H.Q. of Coys. in the line.
	2.	,, Btns. ,,
	3.	,, Coys. in support.
LEFT GROUP.	1.	H.Q. of Coys. in the line.
	2.	H.Q. of Btns. ,,
	3.	Support line of Rt. Coy., Rt. Btn.
	4.	,, Rt. & Left Coy. Left Btn.
	5.	Chateau Redoubt.

CO-OPERATION with HEAVY ARTILLERY.

The Heavy Artillery usually man the following O.P's:-

6" Hows.	SAVOY
6" Hows.	COALBOX
60-prs.	SCHOOLHOUSE
O.P. Exchange	S 2 A 4.6
	F 4 B 8.9.

--------oOo--------

SECRET   Appendix .

37th DIVISIONAL ARTILLERY ORDERS
for -

G A S. In the event of a discharge of gas by the enemy, the Batteries which shoot on the front from where the gas is issuing, will fire on that front at the rate of 2 rounds per 18-pr. gun and 1 round per 4.5" Howitzer per minute.

18-pr batteries should use enfilade fire where possible, otherwise they will barrage NO MAN's LAND when safe to do so. If this is unsafe they will fire on the front line trenches. Shrapnel and H.E. mixed should be fired by the 18-pr. batteries.

Neighbouring batteries will stand by ready to open fire on an attack should the enemy attempt to leave his trenches.

The orders for passing the Gas alarm will be the same as for S.O.S. except that the word "GAS" will be used instead of the letters "S.O.S." In addition gongs will be rung and Klaxon horns blown.

HOSTILE BOMBARDMENT. In the event of a severe hostile bombardment, our batteries covering the front bombarded will shell the enemy trenches opposite. Rate of fire and flank support will be as for a Gas attack.

                                                   Sd/- CECIL M.H. STEVENS, Major,

6.1.1917.   Bde.Major, 37th Divl. Artillery.

Copies to-
- 37 Divn.   Right Group
- XI Corps R.A.   Left Group
- XI Corps H.A.   D.O.T.B.
- 56 Div. Arty.
- 5th Div. Arty.
- 37 Div. Arty.
- Staff Captain.

SECRET

Arrangements for H.A. Support in the event of S.O.S. Calls on 37th Division Front.

1. NEUVE CHAPELLE SECTION.

    (a) S.O.S. "NEUVE CHAPELLE LEFT" (Boundaries SIGNPOST LANE
                                                    to HUN STREET.)

    ```
    150 S.B. (N)    S 5 D 70.45.        (1  6" How)
    204 S.B.        S 5 B 95.38         (1  6" How)
                    S 11 A 95.60        (1  6" How)
      9 H.B.        S 6 A 50.05         (2  60-prs)
    ```

    (b) S.O.S. "NEUVE CHAPELLE RIGHT"   (Boundaries HUN STREET)
                                        (to BOND STREET.   )

    ```
      9 H.B.        S 11 B 1½.2½        (1  60-pr.)
                    S 11 C 1½.3         (1  60-pr.)
                   (NORA TRENCH         (1  60-pr.)
                   (S 16 B 6.0
    ```

2. FERME DU BOIS SECTION.

    (a) S.O.S. "BOIS LEFT"   (Boundaries ROPE STREET to
                                            BOND STREET SOUTH).

    ```
    204 S.B.        S 16 A 9.3.         (1  6" How)
                    S 22 B 0.8          (1  6" How)
    2 London H.B.  (ADALBERT ALLEY      (2  4.7" guns)
                   (S 22 D 40.35
      9 H.B.       NORA TRENCH, S 16 B 6.0   (2  60-prs.)
    ```

    (b) S.O.S. "BOIS RIGHT"   (Boundaries ROPE STREET to
                                            LOTHIAN ROAD).

    ```
    204 S.B.        S 22 C 9.3.         (1  6" How)
                    S 28 A 78.25        (1  6" How).
    2 London H.B.  (EITEL ALLEY SOUTH   (1  4.7" gun).
                   (S 28 B 65.80
                    S 28 B 5.2.         (1  4.7" gun).
    ```

SECRET   VISUAL SIGNALLING SCHEME   C/125/5

RIGHT   A/124.   Signalling has been tested by lamp from LADDER HOUSE
GROUP   (S 9 C 85.05) and also from Left Btn. H.Qs. directly to the
                 Orchard on the Left of the Battery.

        B/124   (a)   Visual signalling could be carried out from the
                      road below BREWERY O.P. (S 20 D 3.4) to corner of
                 road (S 25 B 75.70) thence by lamp to house at X 29 D 85.25,
                 then by flag or runner to the Battery.

                (b)   From Company Headquarters to O.P. by lamp.

        C/124.   Visual signalling could be carried out from WHITE
                 HART O.P. (S 15 A 2.4) or Btn. H.Qrs. to house in
                 RICHEBOURG (S 2 C 37.15), thence by telephone or runner to Bty.

        D/123.   Visual signalling has been tested from the WHITE
                 HART O.P. to a place on the left of the Battery, thence
                 by telephone to the battery.

                 This country is so flat that it does not lend itself
                 to visual signalling. For communication between Batteries and
                 H.Qrs. one would need in every case at least one intermediate
                 station, and in some cases two or three.

LEFT   1.   NEUVE CHAPELLE RIGHT.
GROUP.   A/123 from MOORHEN O.P.   )   to LANSDOWNE HOUSE O.P. - Btn.
             A/126 from WINTER POST O.P.)   Hqrs. by shutter, flag or lamp.
             D/126 observes at LANSDOWNE HOUSE O.P.
        From LANSDOWNE HOUSE O.P. - direct to A/126 and D/126 & from
        A/126 to A/123 all by flag or lamp and in the latter case by
        shutter as well.
        This has been worked successfully, but the hole in rear of the
        turret of LANSDOWNE HOUSE O.P. requires widening, and a crow's
        nest at M 32 C 9.7 (A/126) is being constructed under R.E.
        supervision.
                 In the event of a bombardment, 2 runners per battery
        are provided at each Battery O.P., and 2 runners in addition
        per 18-pr. battery at LANSDOWNE HOUSE.

        II. NEUVE CHAPELLE LEFT.
             B/123 from PORT ARTHUR O.P.   )   by runner to M 34 C 7.8
             B/123 from HEATH ROBINSON O.P.)   Battalion Headquarters.
             C/123 from M 34 C 70.25 O.P.   )
                 from M 34 C 7.8 to disused gun position M 33 A 8.8 by
                         Lamp, Flag and Shutter.
                 from M 34 C 7.8 to St. VAAST HOUSE S 3 A 0.9, lamp &
                                                                flag.
                 from M 33 A 8.8   to B & C/126, lamp, flag &
                                                              shutter.
                 from St. VAAST HOUSE to B/123, lamp, flag and shutter.
        NOTE... M 33 A 8.8 & St. VAAST HOUSE connect by lamp or flag and
                 possibly shutter as well.
        In the event of a bombardment, 2 runners per battery are
        provided both at O.P's and at Battalion Headquarters in
        M 34 C 7.8.

                            Sd/- CECIL M.H. STEVENS, Major,
                                 Bde.Major, 37th Divl. Artillery.
        15.1.17.

A 8 B ½.1¾	B		Z. House.
A 8 C 7½.4	B		Winter Palace
A 8 C 8.4¼	B		Pringle's Pride
A 9 C 8½.4			Queens Bomb Store
A 9 C 9.4½	B		Fentons Folly
A 9 C 6½.4½	B		Belle Vue
A 9 C 7.2½	B		Sappers House
A 15 A 4½.7½	B		B. House
A 15 C 9.9			Spoil Bank
A 14 B 6.0	B		Distillery Pont Fixe
A 15 C 5.6¼	S		The Needle. Hun View.
A 15 C 5.6½	S		The Needle
A 15 C 6.3	B		Kingsclere
A 15 C 8.1	B	B	Sannas House (1 & 2)
A 21 A 2½.1	B	B	Mountain House (1 & 2)
A 20 D 9.7.	B		Braddell Point
A 20 D 9.7	B		Braddell Castle
A 20 D 7¾.6¾	B		The Tower of Babel (1 & 2)
A 20 D 5¼.6¼	B		The Ruin
A 20 D 7¾.6¼	S		The Curragh
A 21 C 4.7½	B		The White House
A 20 D 8½.6½	B		The Four hundred.
A 20 D 7½.4¾	B		O.P.Unnamed
A 20 D 7.4¼	B		The Babe
A 20 D 7½.2¼	S		Wilsons House
A 20 D 7½.2	B		Greenwood House.
A 20 D 8½.6¼	B		O.P. in Brickstack.
A 20 D 7¼.1	S		Ridge House.
A 26 B 5.4½			Maison Rouge
G 8 D 8.3			Vermelles Water Tower.
F 29 C 4.2			Fosse 9.
H 20 A 2.2			Fosse 3.

Map reference 1/10,000.

O. P's on XI Corps Front.

N 8 A 2.5	B.S.	Bristol	
N 7 D 4¼.6¼	B	Cottages	
N 13 A 8½.8½	b	Snowden	
N 13 A 8.8	B	Siege House	
N 13 A 9½.6½	B	Tea Shop	
N 13 A 5½.4	B	Farm	
M 18 D 7.3½	B	Fauquissart Post	
M 17 B 5.3½		Pear Tree O.P. (approx.)	
M 18 C 9½.4	B	C .R.A's House.	
M 18 D 2½.2	B	Convent	
M 18 D 3.0	B	Lounge	
M 22 B 8½.5¼	B	Peak	
M 22 D 1½.5½	B	The Min	
M 23 D 3½.2½		Stink Farm	
M 24 C ½.4	B	Avington Park	
M 24 C 1.3	B	Chapigny	
M 29 C 9.9	B	Moated Grange	
M 28 D 8½.2¼	B	Criccieth Castle	
M 35 A 9.9 (approx.)		Camouflage Tree	
M 35 C 9.4½	B	Chateau Redoubt	37 Divn
M 35 D 0.3	B	Cavendish Sq.,Haymarket	
M 35 D 1.2¾		Camouflage Tree.	37 Div.
S 5 A 5.8½	B	Heath Robinsons Ho.	,,
M 34 C 7.2½	B	Pont Logy No.2.	,,
M 34 C 6½.5	B	Pont Logy No.1.	,,
S 3 A 0.9	B	St. Vaast O.P.	,,
S 5 A 5.5	B	Boot Factory.	,,
S 3 D 8.9	B	Lansdowne Post	,,
S 5 C 0.1½	B	Port Arthur	,,
S 10 A 95.40		New Hutch.	,,
S 10 B 2.5½	B	Winters Post.	,,
S 10 B ½.4		96 Piccadilly	,,
S 10 A 9¼.3	B	Streiff's House	,,
S 9 D 9¼.6½	B	Moorhen	,,
S 9 D 9½.6½	S	Gaiety	,,
S 9 D 9¼.6	B	Pete's Post	,,
S 9 D 8½.5½	B	Leicester Lounge	,,
S 9 D 7.6	B B B	Factory	,,
S 9 D 8.3	B	Maxim House	,,
S 9 D 4.3½	B	Corner House	,,
S 9 D 2.3	B	Station E.	,,
S 9 D 2.2	B	Pump House	,,
S 9 C 9.1	B	Savoy	,,
S 9 C 8½.0	B	Ladder House	,,
S 15 A 4.6	B	The Nook	,,,
S 15 A 3½.5½	B	Barricade House	,,
S 15 A 1.3	B	Trocadero	,,
S 15 A ¼.3¼	B	White Hart	,,
S 15 A 2.1	B	Cadbury	,,
S 15 C 4.0	B	The Oven	,,
S 15 C 3¾.0	B	Coal box	,,
S 20 D 3.2½	B	Brewery.	,,
S 20 D 2.1½	B	Gun House	
S 20 C 8½.2½	B	Bell House.	
S 20 C 7¼.½	B	Dressing Station	
S 25 B 7¾.7	B	Corner House	
S 27 A 7.3½	B	Canot Farm or Welsh Harp	
S 25 D 6.6½	S	Insurance Office	
S 25 D 5¼.5	B	No.39	
S 25 D 7½.3½	B	Rectory	
S 25 D 8½.2½	B	Butchers Shop	
S 25 D 5.1	B	Girls School	
S 26 C 3.3	B	School House	
A 1 B 8½.0	B	Convent	
A 2 C 3.6½	B	Cleveland House	
A 2 C 3.4	B.S.	(27 Le Plantin) (Maison Riche.)	
A 8 A 8.8	B	Harley House	
A 8 A 8.7½	B.B	Heytesbury House (1 & 2)	
A 8 A 9¾.3¾	B	"V" House.	
A 8 A 8.7		The Langham.	

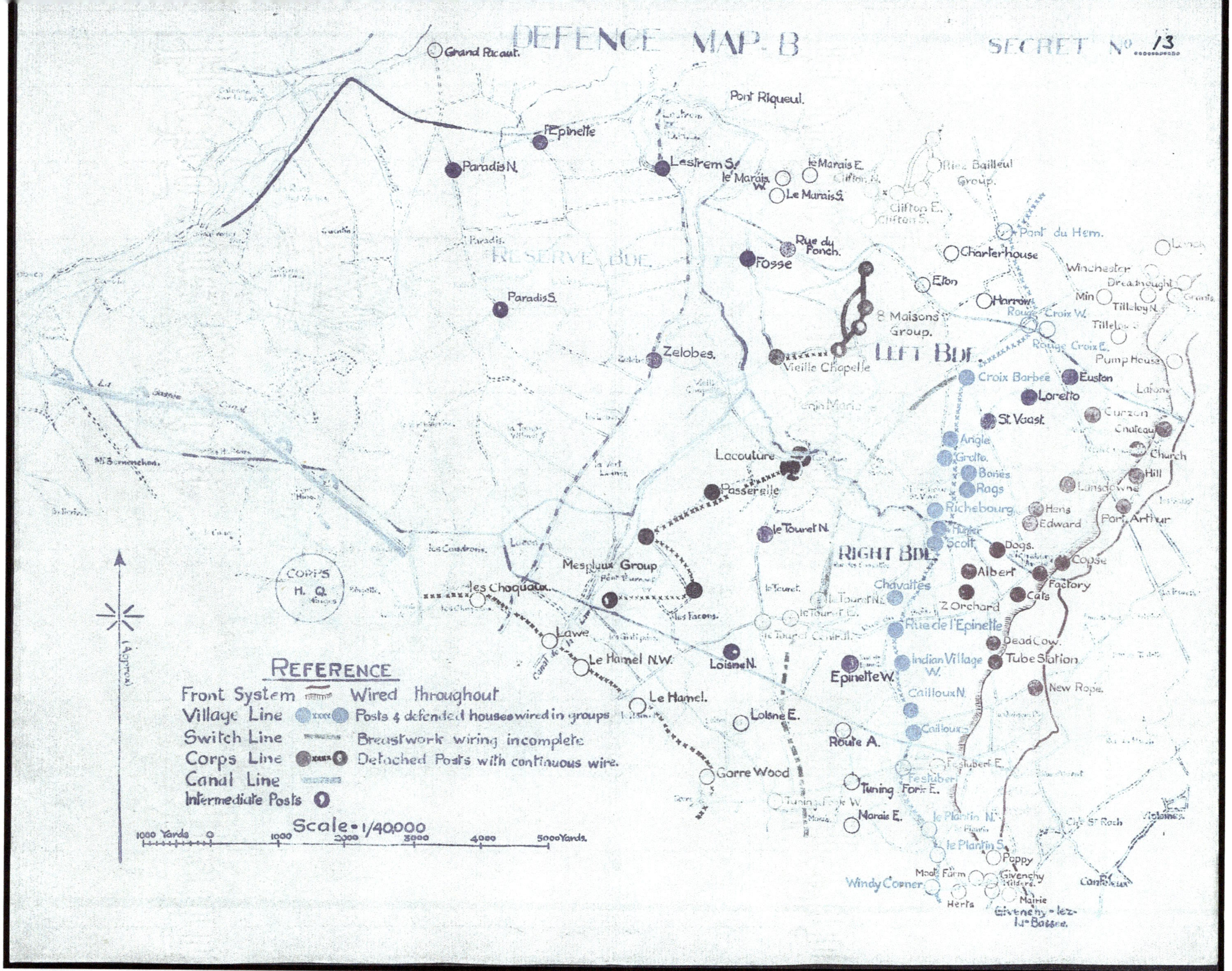

DEFENCE MAP B
SECRET No. 13
Grand Ricaut.
Pont Riqueul.
l'Epinette
Paradis N.
Lestrem S.
le Marais W.
le Marais E.
Le Marais S.
Riez Bailleul Group.
Clifton E.
Pont du Hem.
Charterhouse
Rue du Ponch.
Fosse
RESERVE BDE.
Paradis S.
Eton
Harrow
Winchester
Dreadnought
Min
Tilleloy N.
Rouge Croix W.
Rouge Croix E.
8 Maisons Group.
Zelobes.
Vieille Chapelle
LEFT BDE.
Pump House
Croix Barbee
Euston
Loretto
St. Vaast
Curzon
Chateau
Church
Hill
Angle
Grotto.
Bones
Rags
Richebourg
Lansdowne
Hens
Edward
Port Arthur
Lacouture
Passerelle
le Tourret N.
Scott
Dogs.
Albert
Copse
Factory
RIGHT BDE.
Chavattes
Cats
Z Orchard
Mesplaux Group
les Choquaux.
les Facons.
Lawe
Rue de l'Epinette
Dead Cow.
Tube Station
Le Hamel N.W.
Loisne N.
Epinette W.
Indian Village W.
New Rope.
Cailloux N.
Le Hamel.
Loisne E.
Route A.
Cailloux
Festubert E.
Festubert
Garre Wood
Tuning Fork E.
Marais E.
le Plantin N.
le Plantin S.
Poppy
Moat Farm
Givenchy
Windy Corner
Herts
Mairie
Givenchy-lez-la-Bassee.
Cuinchy
CORPS H. Q.
(Approx)
REFERENCE
Front System — Wired throughout
Village Line — Posts & defended houses wired in groups
Switch Line — Breastwork wiring incomplete
Corps Line — Detached Posts with continuous wire.
Canal Line
Intermediate Posts
Scale - 1/40,000
1000 Yards 0 1000 2000 3000 4000 5000 Yards.

SECRET

DIRECTORY.

I. **XIth Corps** --- Headquarters at HINGES.
G.O.C. General Sir Robert Haking
G.O.C.R.A. Brigadier General Carey.
Staff Officer R.A. Major Oldham.

II. XIth Corps --- Headquarters at FOSSE near LESTREM.
    Heavy   Brigadier General Crampton
    Arty.   Brigade Major Captain McIver.

III. 53rd Heavy --- Officer Commanding..Lt Col.Wynter
    Arty   Headquarters at...R 31 D 8.8
    Group.

IV. Divn.on Right - 5th Division Headquarters at BETHUNE
G.O.C. Major General Stephens
C.R.A. Brig.Genl.Hussey.
Brigade Major Captain Wallace.

V. Division on -- 56th Division Headquarters at La GORGUE.
   Left.   G.O.C. Major General Hull
C.R.A. Brig.Genl.Elkington
Brigade Major..Major Don.

VI. 10th Squadron, Headquarters at CHATEAU L'ABBAYE near CHOCQUES.
    R.F.C.   O.C.   Captain Ward.

VII. 10th Kite --- Section Headquarters at R 20 C 6.6
    Balloon Sect.   Coy.Hd.Qrs. at ... ...R 21 C 1.3
    No:2 Coy.   Company Commander ... Captain Roxby.

VIII. Anti-Aircraft. 78th Section, A Battery, Anti-Aircraft Artillery.
Section Headquarters at Les FACONS, X 15 C 65.60
Section Commander Lieut Evans, R.A.
Position of guns ... X 25 D 50.45
    Section B Battery, Anti-aircraft Artillery.
Position of Guns ... M 31 B 4.6
Battery Headquarters at BOUT DEVILLE
Section Commander .. Lieut. Marryat.

IX. First Army   Headquarters at LILLERS.
    Field Survey O.C.   Major Wilbraham
    Company.

X. Resting Inf.Bde. Headquarters att VIEILLE CHAPELLE

XI. I.O.M.   No:21 Workshop at La GORGUE

               No: 7 Workshop at BETHUNE
                   I.O.M. in charge of both...Capt.Glanville
                                        at La GORGUE.

17.1.17.

SECRET

LIST of POSITION CALLS

shewing Batteries occupying the Positions

Batty.	Nature of Position.		Office Position.	Position Call.
	Right Group H.Q.		X 16 D 8.0	CD 84
	Left Group H.Q.		R 29 C 1.5.	DB 81
	Battery Position		S 7 D 90.65	CD 20
A/124	(Right Group).		M 31 C 50.25	DA 24
,, Sect.	,,		F 5 B 45.25	CB 73
B/124	,,		F 18 A 38.85	CA 57
,, Sect.	,,		S 1 D 38.60	DA 35
C/124	,,		X 17 D 9.7.	CD 21
D/123	,,		X 30 C 55.40	CC 54
D/124	,,		X 24 C 25.60	CC 77
D/15 Sect.	Battery Position			
A/28	(Left Group).		M 32 C 9.7.	DA 29
,, Sect.	,,		X 18 A 8.6	CD 54
A/282	,,		M 26 D 5.5.	DB 82
,, Sect.	,,		M 23 A 25.85	DB 83
A/123	,,		S 1 B 4.4.	DA 23
,, Sect.	,,		S 19 D 20.86	CC 21
B/123	,,		S 2 A 67.51	DA 79
,, Sect.	,,		S 14 C 85.82	CD 89
D/123 ,,	,,		M 32 B 4.3	DA 80
,, Sect.	,,		M 27 A 1.1	DB 31
D/282 ,,	,,		M 33 A 9.6.	DA 75
NAME				
LADDER HOUSE	Observation Post.		S 9 C 83.15	CD 22
STOCKTON LODGE	,,		S 9 D 65.52	Cd 71
PUMP HOUSE	,,		S 9 D 10.20	CD 63
BREWERY	,,	RIGHT	S 20 D 30.25	CC 63
CANNON HOUSE	,,		S 27 A 8.4	CC 65
WHITE HART	,,	GROUP	S 15 A 2.4	CD 25
TROCADERO	,,		S 15 A 05.35	CD 62
OVEN	,,		S 15 C 40.05	CD 73
SAVOY	,,		S 9 C 8.1	
BARRICADE HOUSE	,,		S 15 A 35.55	CD 61
WINTERS POST	,,		S 10 B 25.43	CD 38
LANSDOWNE HOUSE	,,		S 3 D 8.9	DA 74
HEATH ROBINSON HOUSE	,,	LEFT	M 35 C 55.15	DA 32
FACTORY	,,		S 9 D 60.55	CD 23
MOORHEN	,,	GROUP	S 9 D 8.5.	CD 68
PORT ARTHUR.	,,		S 4 D 8.2	DA 31
	D.O.T.M., H.Q.		S 7 D 5.3.	CD 35
	Medium T.M.Billet		S 8 B 3.3	CD 36
Y/37	,, ,,		S 9 D 25.78	CD 37
X/37	,, ,,		S 21 D 10.85	CC 23
Z/37	,, ,,		M 35 C 50.15	DA 30

FIELD COMPANIES, R.E.

Dispatch

Right Group
Left Group.

    Field Companies will work with Brigades as follows:- *For OP's.*

152nd Coy. ... ... HUITS MAISONS .. to work
O.C. Capt.Hanna   with our
                                                               LEFT GROUP.

153rd Coy. ... ... LE TOURET .. to work
O.C.Lieut.Weeks.   with our
                                               RIGHT GROUP.

1st January, 1917.      Major
                              Brigade Major, 37th Divl. Arty.

153 Fueld Co. will do work for all Divl Arty behind the OP line.

WAR DIARY
or
INTELLIGENCE SUMMARY.
(Erase heading not required.)

Army Form C. 2118.

February 1917

Place	Date	Hour	Summary of Events and Information	Remarks and references to Appendices
	1st.		Enemy bombarded our front and support trenches in S10 b & d with T.M.s - very little damage was done. Relief of 37 Div C.R.A. by the 5th 15.6" Div Arty commenced tonight. See Appendix 73	App 73.
	2nd.		1/2 Relief completed, brigades remaining in wagon lines.	App 74
	3rd.		
	12/13.		37 D.A. commenced relief of 24 D.A. in LOOS. 14 B/S and HULLUCH Sections.	
	13/14		Relief completed. CRA 37 D.A. took over 10 am 14th. Very quiet day. 108 A.F.A Brigade is grouped tactically under 37 D.A. H.Q. R.A. 37 Div opened at BRACQUEMONT.	
	14th		9.15 p.m. to 10.30 p.m. enemy bombarded our trenches in M5 d & M6 c - Right Group fired effectively on barrage lines. Bombardment was lifted from 12.15 am to 12.37 am. Enemy fired red rockets which were answered by his S.O.S. signals.	
	15th		Quiet day, except for the usual T.M. activity. Opposite to Left Group communications and back areas were swept during the night, a relief being suspected opposite too	

WAR DIARY
or
INTELLIGENCE SUMMARY.
(Erase heading not required.)

Army Form C. 2118.

Place	Date	Hour	Summary of Events and Information	Remarks and references to Appendices
	16th		Nothing to report	
	17"		Quiet day.	
	18"		Nothing to report. V/37 A.T.M. when fired on by enemy H.T.M. immediately replied, after eight bombs each	
	19th		V/37 landed its eighth into enemy's shaft, it exploded inside blowing large beams + debris into the air, destroying it completely.	
	20th		Usual enemy T.M. activity along Divisional front. Two A.T.M.'s were silenced by V/37 T.M. and D/123. in H.13.D.40.20. and H.13.D.40.50. We carried out a dummy raid bombardment at night. Retaliation was practically nil, some machine gun fire and rifle grenades fell on our front line. M.5.B. + D only 30 H.E. 10.5 cm fell in some locality. Wire was successfully cut at H.25.c.95.05 and A.31.B.10.90 by V/37 T.M. battery, results reported by patrols.	
	21st		Nothing to report. Weather very misty. Enemy quiet except T.M. activity, he also dropped 50 lb. shell near A/123 doing no damage & inflicting no casualties, and 30 S of Vermelles.	
	22.		Weather too misty for any observation. Nothing to report.	
	23		Nothing to report.	
	24		Usual artillery activity, enemy quiet except for his T.M. fire.	
	25		Nothing to report.	

WAR DIARY
or
INTELLIGENCE SUMMARY.
(Erase heading not required.)

Army Form C. 2118.

Place	Date	Hour	Summary of Events and Information	Remarks and references to Appendices
	Feb'y 26		Usual activity on both sides. Enemy shows signs of nervousness – is easily silenced by our retaliations.	
	27 28		Enemy artillery very quiet. Dummy Raid with Gas took place 10pm. Enemy retaliated vigorously at 7.0pm. Gas was discharged on our front line at 9.15pm. T.M.'s & M.G.'s in our watching co-operated from 9.8pm. from Nukkruct sector – our artillery – Results are unknown.	App 75 App 7/5 76

SECRET   Copy No. 14

App 73

37th DIVISIONAL ARTILLERY

OPERATION ORDER No. 46

1. The 37th Division will be withdrawn from the line, into G.H.Q. Reserve. The withdrawal will be completed by daylight on 2/3rd February, after which all units will be held ready to move by road or rail at 9 hours notice.
   As soon as possible all vehicles will be kept ready packed.

2. The Left Group front will be taken over by the 56th Divisional Artillery and the Right Group front by the 5th Divisional Artillery.

3. Guns and Howitzers will be withdrawn and retained. Four guns per battery on the night of 1/2nd Feby. and 2 guns per battery on the night of 2/3rd Feby. The relieving batteries will bring their guns up to the Wagon Lines of the Batteries that are being relieved. The 37th Divisional Artillery will take the guns up to the positions, and withdraw their own with the same teams. Reliefs will take place after dark.

4. Medium Trench Mortars, complete with beds will be removed. The H.T.M. will be handed over to the 56th Divl. Arty.

5. Group & Battery Commanders of the 5th and 56th Divisional Artillery will be at the Right & Left Group Headquarters respectively of the 37th Divl. Artillery at 10 a.m. on the 1st February. The D.O.T.M's of the above Divisions will meet the D.O.T.M., 37th Division at his Headquarters at the same hour.
   All details will be arranged mutually.

6. On withdrawal, batteries, with the exception of D/123 Bde. RFA will concentrate at their respective Wagon Lines. D/123 will move at once into Wagon Lines near PARADIS MILL.

7. The relieving units will take over all ammunition dumped within their areas.
   Those emplacements occupied by the 37th Divl. Artillery, but not re-occupied by the relieving Groups, will be handed over to them, together with the ammunition dumped there.
   The 37th Div. Arty. will supply and account for ammunition up to 10 a.m. on Feby. 3rd.
   Receipts for all ammunition handed over will be taken. Echelons will move out full, in the proportion of 75 A & 25 AX.

8. C.R.A. 37th Div. Arty. will hand over to C.R.A's of 5th and 56th Div. Arty. at 10 a.m. on Feby. 3rd at which hour Group Commanders will also hand over.
   37th D.A.H.Q. will remain at LESTREM.

9. All Intelligence Maps and 1/20,000 and 1/10,000 maps will be handed over. A list of those handed over will be forwarded to this Office.
   All aeroplane photos, panoramas, O.P. log books, Arty. Boards and Intelligence books, will also be handed over.
   Artillery Boards of vacant positions should be returned to First Army Field Survey Coy.

10. Table of Reliefs is attached.

                                   Sd/- CECIL M.H. STEVENS, Major,
31.1.17.   Bde. Major, 37th Divl. Artillery.

For distribution see overleaf.

SECRET

TABLE OF RELIEFS.

RIGHT GROUP, 37th Div. Arty.　　　　　　　　　　　　　　　5th Div. Arty.

			Night of		
A/124	Main Position	2 Guns	1/2nd	by	123rd Batty.
A/124	Enfilade Section	2 ,,	1/2nd	,,	,,
A/124	Main Position	2 ,,	2/3rd	,,	,,
B/124	Main Position	2 ,,	1/2nd	,,	124th Batty.
B/124	Enfilade Section	2 ,,	1/2nd	,,	,,
B/124	Main Position	2 ,,	2/3rd	,,	,,
C/124	Position	4 ,,	1/2nd	,,	A/28 A.F.A.
C/124	-	2 ,,	2/3rd	,,	,,
D/123 Sect. at X 17 D 9.7.		2 Hows.	1/2nd	,,	65th Batty.

-o-o-o-o-o-o-o-o-o-o-o-o-o-o-o-o-o-o-o-o-o-o-o-o-o-o-o-o-

LEFT GROUP, 37th Div. Arty.　　　　　　　　　　　　　　　56th DIV. ARTY.

A/282	M 26 D.	4 Guns	Remains.	by	Nil.
A/28	Main	2 ,,	Night of 1/2nd	,,	C/282 A.F.A.
A/28	Enfilade	2 ,,	1/2nd	,,	No relief. position vacated
A/28	Main	2 ,,	2/3rd	,,	C/282 A.F.A.
A/123	Main	3 ,,	1/2nd	,,	B/282 ,,
A/123	Enfilade	1 ,,	1/2nd	,,	B/282 ,,
A/123	Main	2 ,,	2/3rd	,,	B/282 ,,
B/123	Main	3 ,,	1/2nd	,,	C/282 ,,
B/123	Enfilade	1 ,,	1/2nd	,,	No relief. position vacated
B/123	Main	2 ,,	2/3rd	,,	No relief. ,,
D/123	M 32 B	2 ,,	1/2nd	,,	D/282 A.F.A.
D/123	M 27 A	2 ,,	2/3rd	,,	D/282 ,,
D/282	M 33 A.	2 ,,	Remains	,,	Nil.

------------------------oOo------------------------

SECRET   aH 74   Copy No: 16

37th Divisional Artillery Operation

Order No: 47

Ref. Map
BETHUNE (Combined Sheet)
1/40,000.

I. The 37th Division will relieve the 24th Division, 1st Corps in the LOOS - 14 BIS and HULLOCH Sections, the relief being completed by midnight 13/14th February, 1917.

II. The line will be taken over by Infantry Brigades as under:-

112th Infantry Brigade - RIGHT SECTION (LOOS) H.Q. L 35 A 5.2.
63rd   ,,   ,,   - CENTRE SECTION (14 BIS) H.Q. L 23 C 8.0.
111th   ,,   ,,   - LEFT SECTION (HULLOCH) H.Q. G 13 D 2.4.

III. Artillery reliefs will be carried out on nights 12/13th and 13/14th February in accordance with attached Table "A", the 37th Div. Arty. taking its own guns into action.
  Trench Mortar reliefs to be completed by midnight 13/14th under mutual arrangements between D.T.M.O's.
  24th Div. Arty. will hand over the 3 surplus M.T.M's in their possession and 4 H.T.M's with stores and indents for deficiencies.
  At least 25 and 30 rounds per T.M. will be left at each Medium and Heavy emplacement.

IV. The Divisional front will be covered by the 37th Div. Art. and the 108th A.F.A. Brigade (less 2 batteries 18-prs. and 1 Section Hows. at present attached to 6th Division).
  The 108th A.F.A. Brigade will remain in present positions. and will be attached to 37th Divl. Artillery.

RIGHT GROUP covering
  RIGHT SECTION.   Col. W.H. Drake,   H.Q. L 35 A 4.2
                    C.M.G., R.F.A.
                    (108th A.F.A. Bde. (less 2 Btys. 18-prs. & 1 Sect.
                    (Hows.
                    (4 18-prs. 123rd Bde. R.F.A., 4 18-prs. 124 Bde.
                    (R.F.A.
                    (2 Hows. 123rd Bde. R.F.A., 2 Hows. 124 Bde. RFA.

Centre Group covering
  CENTRE SECTION.   Col. H. Rouse, ...H.Q., L 23 D 1.7.
                    C.B., D.S.O., R.F.A.
                    124th Bde. R.F.A. (less guns lent to Right Sect.)

Left Group covering
  LEFT SECTION.   Col. Hope Johnstone, R.F.A.. H.Q., G 13 D 2.5.
                    123rd Bde. R.F.A. (less guns lent to Right Sect.)

  In the event of the return (previous to the relief) of the guns and howitzers belonging to the 108th A.F.A. Bde. at present attached to the 6th Div. Arty., these guns and howitzers will replace the guns and howitzers of the 106th and 107th Brigades, R.F.A. at present attached to the Right Group. Under these conditions the 124th Brigade, R.F.A. (complete) will relieve the Centre Group and the 123rd F.A. Brigade (complete) will relieve the Left Group.

V. Batteries will take over all maps, battery boards, aeroplane photographs, logbooks, switchboards, communications, Trench Stores, etc. in their respective positions. Existing Defence Schemes, Mutual support, Barrages, etc. will remain in force.

VI. Advance parties consisting of one F.O.O. and two telephonists per battery will proceed to new area by Motor lorry on the 11th inst.
    Two lorries will be at LOCON CROSS ROADS (X 7 A) at 9 a.m. on above date.
    Battery Commanders, and battery and D.A.C. representatives for reconnoitring Wagon lines can avail themselves of these lorries, returning in the evening.

VII. Echelons will move full. All ammunition dumps at Gun positions will be taken over by incoming batteries.
    Echelons of outgoing batteries, 24th Divisional Artillery, will be filled up by 37th Divisional Artillery opposite numbers.
    Separate instructions are being issued with regard to details of ammunition exchange and supply.
    D.A.C. 24th Division will be responsible for the supply of ammunition up to 12 noon, 13th February, at which time 37th D.A.C. takes over.

VIII. Command of Divisional area passes to G.O.C. 37th Division at 4 p.m. 13th February, at which time D.H.Q. will close at LESTREM and reopen at BRAQUEMONT (L 25 B 2.8).
    C.R.A. 37th Division will assume command of the Artillery covering the Divisional front at 10 a.m. 14th February, at which time D.A.H.Q. will close at LESTREM and reopen at BRAQUEMONT (L 25 B 0.1)

IX. Completion of reliefs to be reported each night to this office.

X. ACKNOWLEDGE.

Issued at 8pm.
10th Feby/1917.   Brigade Major, 37th Divl. Arty.
                                                         Major

Copies to:-
No:		
1	I Corps, R.A.	9..124 Bde. R.F.A.
2	XI Corps, R.A.	10..37th D.A.C.
3	XI Corps Heavy Arty.	11..D.O.T.M.
4	37th Div.	12..A.P.M. 37 Div.
5	37th Div.Q	13..A.P.M. BETHUNE
6	5th Div. Arty.	14..Town Majr. BETHUNE
7	56th Div. Arty.	15..Staff Capt.
8	123 Bde. R.F.A.	16 & 17 Diary.

TABLE "A"

Date	Units	From	To Wagon Lines.	Relieve	Position	Remarks.
12th Feb.	2 Sects. A/123	Present W.Lines	L 19 C 25.20	2 Sects. A/106	G 14 B 10.25)	
	2 Sects. B/123	Present W.Lines	K 24 D 95.90	2 Sects. B/106	C 27 A 7.1)	
	2 Sects. C/123	Present W.Lines	L 19 C 60.09	2 Sects. C/106	G 32 C 1.2)	Arriving at new Wagon
	2 Sects. D/123	Present W.Lines	L 25 A 30.80	1 Sect. D/106	G 27 C 8.4)	Lines at 4 p.m.
				1 Sect. D/106	M 2 D 1.5)	All reliefs to take
						place after dark under
	2 Sects. A/124	Present W.Lines	L 19 A 30.40	1 Sect. A/107	G 27 C 0.1)	arrangements to be made
				1 Sect. A/107	N 2 B 3.5)	between battery Command
	2 Sects. B/124	Present W.Lines	L 31 A 60.62	2 Sects. B/107	G 33 A 75.50)	-ers concerned.
	2 Sects. C/124	Present W.Lines	L 25 A 60.90	2 Sects. C/107	G 26 D 60.25)	
	2 Sects. D/124	Present W.Lines	L 33 B 40.80	1 Sect. D/107	G 32 D 8.2)	
				1 Sect. D/107	G 32 D 25.20)	
13th Feb.	37th D.A.C.	Present W.Lines	W.L.of 24th D.A.C.	24th D.A.C.	K 15 B	To be in Wagon Lines
					E 25 D	by 11 a.m.
	Remaining Sects. of batteries 123rd and 124th Bdes. R.F.A.	Present W.Lines	W.Lines 106th and 107th Bdes. R.F.A.	Complete reliefs		

NOTE. Co-ordinates are approximate only.
March Orders issued separately.

SECRET

Ref: Map
BETHUNE (Combined Sheet)
1/40,000

MARCH ORDERS.

I. Relieving Sections of Batteries of 123rd and 124th F.A.Brigades will march on 12th February to their new Wagon Lines in BRAQUEMONT via BETHUNE and NOEUX LES MINES, going up into action after dark.

II. Remaining Sections of Batteries will march to their new Wagon Lines on 13th February going up into action after dark. (Route as for 12th February).

III. Starting Point - LOCON CROSS ROADS (X 7 A).

IV. On both days sections will march in order of batteries, 123rd F.A.Brigade leading. Heads of columns to pass starting point at 12 noon.
O's.C. Brigades to detail Officers to be in charge of each Brigade on the march.

V. February 12th. 1 Officer and 2 men from each Brigade to be detailed to proceed in advance to superintend traffic of column through BETHUNE.
On this date no Artillery movement to take place in the town of BETHUNE excepting between the hours of 1 p.m. and 3 p.m.
February 13th. O.C. 123rd F.A.Brigade to detail an Officer and 2 men for Traffic duty in BETHUNE.

VI. 37th D.A.C. will march on 13th instant under orders of O.C. so as to be in the new Wagon Lines at HOUCHIN and HESDIGNEUL by 11 a.m. on that date.
O.C., D.A.C. to make arrangements for Traffic Control through BETHUNE.

VII. Two hundred yards distance to be maintained between Units on the march.

VIII. ACKNOWLEDGE.

Issued at 8 p.m.
10th Feby.,1917.

Major,
Bde. Major, 37th Divl. Artillery.

SECRET.   Copy No: 14

37th Divisional Artillery Operation
Order No: 48

Ref.Map
BETHUNE
(Comb.Sheet)
1/40,000

I. The portion of 108th Army F.A. Brigade at present attached to the 6th Division will return into action under the 24th Div. Artillery orders on nights 12/13th – 13/14th February and will relieve the guns and howitzers belonging to the Left and Centre Groups at present attached to the Right Group with the exception of the Section of howitzers belonging to D/107 at G 32 D 25.20 which will be relieved by D/124 Bde.R.F.A. as already arranged.
This Section will remain under the Right Group.

II. The following are the consequent amendments to Operation Order No:47, Table A :-

Under date 12th February
For 2 Sects C/123 ... ...   relieve 2 Sects C/106 at G 32 C 1.2

   read   do.   with go into position at
                                do.   G 14 C 6.1

For 2 Sects D/123 ... ...   relieve (1 Sect.D/106 at G 27 C 8.4
                                    (1 Sect.D/106 at M 2 D 1.5

   read   do.   do. (1 Sect.D/106 at G 27 C 8.4
                                    (1 Sect.D/106 to Reserve Position in G 27 C.

For 2 Sects.A/124 ... ...   relieve(1 Sect.A/107 at G 27 C 0.1
                                   (1 Sect.A/107 at M 2 B 3.5

   read   do.   do. (1 Sect.A/107 at G 27 C 0.1
                                   (1 Sect.A/107 into empty pits G 27 C 0.1.

III. The Left, Centre & Right Sections will thus be covered respectively by the 123rd Bde.R.F.A., the 124th Bde.R.F.A.(less 1 Section Hows.) and the 108th Army F.A.Bde.(plus 1 Sect.Hows. from 124th Bde.R.F.A.

IV.   Acknowledge.

                                              (signed)
                                                           Major
Issued at 8 p.m.
11th February, 1917.   Brigade Major, 37th Divl.Arty.

Copies to:- No:1 I Corps R.A.   6 5th Div.Arty.   11 D.O.T.M.
             2 XI Corps R.A.   7 56th Div.Arty.   12 Staff Capt.
             3 XI Corps H.A.   8 123rd Bde.R.F.A. 13 & 14 Diary.
             4 37th Div.   9 124th Bde.R.F.A. 15 24th DA
             5 37th Div.G.   10 37th D.A.C.

SECRET.

App. 76

C/119/3

37 Div.
G/645/68.

37th Div.Arty.
63rd Inf. Bde.
111th Inf. Bde.
112th Inf. Bde.

1. Gas and smoke will be discharged tonight from 111th Infantry Brigade front. Zero hour for discharge of the Gas will be 7.0 p.m.

2. Zero hour for the Artillery programmes in connection with the dummy raids to be carried out by the 63rd and 111th Infantry Brigades will be 7.5 p.m. tonight.

3. In case it is necessary to postpone the Zero hour for the discharge of Gas for one hour, the code word "DIMINISH" will be sent by telegram from Divisional H.Q. The Zero hour will then be as under:-

   For Gas discharge ... 8.0 p.m.
   For Arty. Programme 8.5 p.m.

4. Should the wind not allow of the discharge of Gas, the code word "CARPET" will be sent. The Artillery programme will then be carried out, starting at a Zero hour which will be notified from these Headquarters by B. A. B. code.

5. No patrols are to go out in front of the line from which Gas is discharges for a period of 6 hours after Zero hour.

6. ACKNOWLEDGE.

27.2.17.

sgd. T.Thompson   Capt.G.S.
            for Lieut.Colonel.
General Staff, 37th Division.

-2-

Right Group
Centre Group
Left Group
D.O.T.M.
1st Can.Div.Arty.
21st Div.Arty.
1st Corps H.A.

For information. Please acknowledge.

27.2.17.

sd/ T.P.Larcom, Major
Bde.Major, 37th Divl.Arty.

SECRET

"R A T S".

PROGRAMME - 28th Feby. - 1st March.

GUNS	OBJECTIVE	TIME TABLE.
4 60prs.) 4 6" Hows.) 8 18 prs.)	H 13 D 32.00 - H 13 B 00.05	Zero plus 5) 18 prs.& 4.5" hows.open with 2 rounds to Zero plus) G.F.and then 2 rounds per gun per min. 26.) HEAVIES & SIEGE ½ round per min.
1 18 pr.) 1 4.5" How.)	Search Comm. Trench from H 19 B 00.78	Zero plus 26) 18 prs. quicken to 3 rounds per gun to Zero plus) per min. 29.
1 18 pr.) 1 4.5" How.)	Search Com. Trench from H 13 D 00.20	Zero plus 29) 18 prs. quicken to 4 rounds per gun to Zero plus) per min, 4.5" Hows. quicken to 3 30.) rounds per gun per minute.
1 18 pr.) 1 4.5" How.)	Search Comm. Trench from H 13 C 95.50	Zero plus 26) HEAVIES & SIEGE 1 round per gun per to Zero plus) min. 34.
1 4.5" How.) 1 4.5" How.) 1 4.5" How.)	H 13 D 22 .62 H 13 D 28.43 H 13 B 00.05	Zero plus 30) 18 prs.& 4.5" Hows. "RUSSIA". to Zero plus) 34.
1 H.T.M.	H 13 D 32.00	

Issued at 6 p.m.
28.2.1917.

signature
Major
Brigade Major, 37th Divl. Artillery.

S.C.1.5.T.
Apr. 75
B.M.
C/118/4

ARTILLERY PROGRAMME, RAID by 63rd INFANTRY BRIGADE, 27th/28th FEBRUARY.

Ref tracing 1/2,500

Phase	Time	Batty.	Guns	Task	Rate of Fire.
-	ZERO	C/124	5	Infantry leave our trenches. Barrage H 31 A 85.92 - H 31 A 92.75	5 Rds. per gun per minute.
-	Zero to Zero plus 4	C/124	5	lift to H 31 B 06.95 - H 31 B 08.80	
-	Zero plus 4 to Zero plus 7	C/124	3	Remain on front trench.	3 Rds. per Gun per minute.
I	Zero to Zero plus 7	E/123	2	H 31 A 96.98 - H 31 B 06.95 (Enfilade)	5 Rds. per Gun per minute.
	"	C/123	4	H 25 D 72.15 - H 31 B 70.60 (Sweep 50')	"
	"	A/124	5	H 25 D 00.24 to comm. trench.	"
	"	C/124	3	(Front trench) H 31 B 12.73.	
	"	A/124	1	Com.Tr. H 25 D 22.08 enfilade.	"
	"	B/124	2	Com.Tr. H 25 D 36.30 enfilade.	"
	"	B/124	2	Com.Tr. H 25 D 36.15 enfilade.	"
	"	F/124	2	Enfilade front trench H 25 D 06.26 to H 25 D 22.33	2 Rds. per How. per minute.
	"	D/123	1	H 25 D 34.25	"
	"	D/123	1	H 25 D 36.15	"
	"	D/124	1	H 25 D 30.04	"
	"	D/124	1	H 31 B 24.72	"
	"	D/124	1	H 31 D 10.25 (O)	"
	"	D/124	1	H 31 D 22.68 (O)	"
-	Zero plus 7	-	-	Front barrage lifts & Raiding Party go in.	
II	Zero plus 7 to Zero plus 30 (or until Raiding Party returns.	B/123	2	H 31 B 25.84 - H 31 B 40.77 (enfilade.)	18prs. 3 rds. per gun per min. for 5 mins. then 2 rds. per gun per min.
		C/124	6)	H 25 D 34.25 - H 31 B 24.72	
		A/124	4)		
		A/124	1	Remain on front trench H 31 B 12.72 (enfilade.)	4.5 Hows. 2 rds. per how per min. throughout.
	Remainder as in Phase I				
-		-	-	Remainder from 1/10,000	

(O) -- HEAVY ARTILLERY :--

Zero till Raiding Party returns.

1 60pr. on Com.Tr. running East from :-
H 25 D 40.11
H 25 D 40.25
H 31 B 70.50

9.2" Hows. :--
H 25 D 67.33
H 25 D 85.21

Note (O) co-ordinates from 1/10,000

NOTE. (O). Co-ordinates from 1/10,000

Signature
BDE. MAJOR,
37TH DIVISIONAL ARTILLERY.

SECRET.   TRENCH MORTAR PROGRAMME.

Reference 1/10,000.

<u>Zero - Z+4.</u>

    1 H.T.M.   H 31 B 18.76)
                 (dug-out)   )
    1 H.T.M.   H 31 B 27.92)
                 (TURKEY)   )   as many rounds
)
<u>Zero+4 - end of Raid.</u>   )   as possible.
)
    1 H.T.M.   H 31 B 70.60)
    1 H.T.M.   H 26 C 20.51)

<u>Zero - end of Raid.</u>

    2" Mortars. H 25 B 55.35)
                H 25 D 75.90)
                H 25 D 30.30)   as many rounds
                H 31 B 31.56)
                H 31 B 30.15)   as possible.
                H 31 D 18.89)
                H 31 D 10.35)

<u>Zero+1 - to end of Raid.</u>

    <u>Stokes.</u>   H 25 B 58.32   H 31 B 15.60   H 31 D 18.59
                H 25 B 62.27   H 31 B 17.53   H 31 D 12.40
                H 25 B 67.17   H 31 B 18.48   H 31 D 10.37
                H 25 B 70.03   H 31 B 22.36   H 31 C 99.31
                H 25 D 72.97   H 31 B 22.22
                H 25 D 68.79   H 31 D 05.95
                H 31 B 13.72   H 31 D 07.85
                H 31 B 23.72   H 31 D 07.73

SECRET   C/116/10

DIVERSION on HULLUCH SECTOR, 27/28th.

TIME	BATTERY	No. of GUNS	TARGET	RATE of FIRE
PHASE I Zero to Zero + 7	2 Sects. A/123) 1 Sect. B/123) 1 Sect. C/123)	8 - 18-prs.	H 19 A 65.60 to H 13 C 55.32.	3 rounds per gun per minute.
	D/123	1 How. 1 How. 1 How. 1 How.	Searching Trench H 13 C 55.32 ,, ,, H 13 C 58.08 ,, ,, H 19 A 65.70 ,, ,, H 19 A 72.50	2 rounds per gun per minute.
PHASE II Zero + 7 to Zero + 12	CEASE FIRING		"Quietness".	
PHASE III Zero + 12 to Zero + 19	Repeat P H A S E I.			
PHASE IV. Zero + 19 to Zero + 23	B/123	1 18-pr. 1 18-pr.	Enfilade H 13 C 58.05 ,, H 19 A 74.49	3 rounds per gun per minute for 3 minutes, then 2 rounds per gun per minute.
	2 Sects. A/123) 1 Sect. C/123)	6 18-prs.	Lift and Barrage :- H 13 D 21.58 to H 15 D 30.02.	
	D/123	1 How. 1 How.	Searching Trench H 13 C 55.32. ,, ,, H 19 B 00.60 to H 13 D 35.02.	2 rounds per How. per minute.
		1 How. 1 How.	Trench junction H 13 C 69.12 ,, H 19 B 04.50	
PHASE V. Zero + 23 to Zero + 27	Repeat P H A S E I.			
PHASE VI. Zero + 27 to Zero + 35.	Repeat P H A S E IV.			
PHASE VII. Zero + 35 to Zero + 37.	Repeat P H A S E I.			

TRENCH MORTARS.

	TIME	No. of GUNS.	TARGET.	Rate of Fire.
PHASE I.	Zero to Zero +7.	4 2" T.M's 1 H.T.M.	H 13 C 58.15 to H 19 A 72.46. H 13 D 35.02.	
PHASE II.	Zero +7 to Zero +12.		CEASE FIRING. "Quietness".	
PHASE III.	Zero +12 to Zero +19.		Repeat PHASE I.	
PHASE IV.	Zero +19 to Zero +23.	1 2" T.M. 1 2" T.M. 1 2" T.M. 1 H.T.M.	Comm. Trench H 19 A 72.50. Enfilade Comm.Trench H 13 C 58.08 Trench junction H 19 B 00.30. As for PHASE I.	
PHASE V.	Zero +23 to Zero +27.		Repeat PHASE I.	
PHASE VI.	Zero +27 to Zero +35.		Repeat PHASE IV.	
PHASE VII.	Zero +35 to Zero +37.		Repeat PHASE I.	

25.2.17.

SECRET
Ra/190

37th Division Q.

Herewith War Diary of 37th Divisional Artillery for the month of March, 1917.

Atkinson Lt RA
for Brigade Major,
31.3.17. for C.R.A., 37th Division.

WAR DIARY
or
INTELLIGENCE SUMMARY.
(Erase heading not required.)

Army Form C. 2118.

Place	Date 1917	Hour	Summary of Events and Information	Remarks and references to Appendices
Haiok	1st		On evening of 1st we carried out a successful Dummy Raid on Right Group front with discharge of gas. The enemy retaliated very feebly.	App 77
-	2nd		Raid on Left Group front took place. The enemy retaliation was feeble coming from a southerly direction. We captured 4 prisoners our casualties consisted of two slightly wounded but brought back + two in on our own trenches. Machine Guns + most trench mortars were successfully kept silent by our bombardment.	App 78
-	3rd		Our artillery was very active shelling back areas, roads, tracks at night, dispersing working parties and snipping. Enemy was more active than usual in last week.	
-	4/5th 5/6th		37 Divisional Artillery relieved by 6th Divisional Artillery. 37th drew out to wagon lines. Two sections per battery relieved first night – one section, second night.	App 79
-	9th 10th		37 Divisional Artillery moved to ANVIN AREA. A.Q. to BERGUETTE. - " - marched to St MICHEL SUR TERNOISE. Headquarters & St MICHEL	App 80
-	16th		- " - moved to GROUCHES area and came under VII Corps on same date. See appendix. – Brigade + D.A.C. came under 1st D.A. Tactically.	App 81
-	19		37 D.A.C. moved to BAVINCOURT	App 82

WAR DIARY
or
INTELLIGENCE SUMMARY.
(Erase heading not required.)

Army Form C. 2118.

Place	Date	Hour	Summary of Events and Information	Remarks and references to Appendices
March	20th		A and B Batteries 124 Brigade marched to SIMENCOURT and to move into action on night 22nd	App 83
—	23rd		Remaining 37 Div. Arty. (C + D batteries 124 Brigade and 123 Bde) moved from GROUCHES to SIMENCOURT.	App 84
—	25		Divisional Arty H.Q. moved to BERNEVILLE	
—	24/25	Night	A + B Batteries /124 Bde sent ½ of each Battery into action under orders of 14th Div. Arty.	
—	25/26 26/27	Night	Remainder of A + B /124 Bde went into action and ½ Btty. of remaining Div Arty of 37 Div. Arty. went into action under orders of 14 Div. Arty.	
—	27/31st		Div. Arty in line North West of BAVRAINS S.E. of ARRAS in our old front system. Work arranged + ordered by 14 Div Arty.	

BDE. MAJOR.
37TH DIVISIONAL ARTILLERY.

SECRET

"R A T S".

PROGRAMME - 26th Feby. - 1st March.

GUNS	OBJECTIVE		TIME TABLE.
4 60prs.) 4 6" Hows.) 8 18 prs.)	H 13 D 32.00 - H 13 B 00.05	Zero plus 5 to Zero plus 26.	18 prs.& 4.5" hows.open with 2 rounds G.F. and then 2 rounds per gun per min. HEAVIES & SIEGE ½ round per min.
1 18 pr.) 1 4.5" How.)	Search Comm. Trench from H 19 B 00.78	Zero plus 26) to Zero plus) 29.	18 prs. quicken to 3 rounds per gun per min.
1 18 pr.) 1 4.5" How.)	Search Comm. Trench from H 13 D 00.20	Zero plus 29) to Zero plus) 30.	18 prs. quicken to 4 rounds per gun per min. 4.5" Hows. quicken to 3 rounds per gun per minute.
1 18 pr.) 1 4.5" How.)	Search Comm. Trench from H 13 C 95.50	Zero plus 26) to Zero plus) 34.	HEAVIES & SIEGE 1 round per gun per min.
1 4.5" How.) 1 4.5" How.) 1 4.5" How.)	H 13 D 22.62 H 13 D 28.43 H 13 B 00.05		
1 H.T.M.	H 13 D 32.00	Zero plus 30) to Zero plus) 34.	18 prs. & 4.5" Hows. "RUSSIA".

Issued at 6 p.m.
26.2.1917.

Major
Brigade Major, 37th Divl. Artillery.

SECRET

9/19/11
App. 78

RIGHT GROUP.

Programme - 2nd March.

Area	TARGET	No. of Guns.			Time & Rate of Fire.
		18-prs.	4.5" Hows.	60-prs.	
Area 1	M 6 D.28.30 and Roadway.	3	2	2	(1) Heavy Group Fire 4 bursts of 3 salvoes between 4 pm. & 13.45 pm. Times to be arranged by O.C.Heavy Group.
Area 2	M 12 B 12.99	3	1	—	
Area 3	M 12 A.90.93 and Roadway.	3	1	1	(2) 18 prs.& 4.5" Hows. Fire 2 rounds G.F. at following hours. 4.30am. - 4.41am - 4.47am. - 4.58am.- 5.10am.-5.2pm - 5.10pm - 5.20pm. 10.2pm - 10.15pm. 5.32 am - 5.45 am
Area 4	M 12 A.84.59 and Roadway.	3	2	1	
Area 5	M 11 B.93.81 to M 12 A. 15.38.	2	—	—	(3) Synchronisation will be arranged by O.C. Right Group.
Area 6	Roadway from Church at M 11 D 40.75 to M 18 A.20.65.	1	—	2	(4) Acknowledge.

2.3.17.

[signature]
Bde.Major,
Major,
Bde.Major, 37th Divl.Artillery.

6 copies Rt Group
6 " Centre }
2 " Rt C'de } = 15 for special.
2 " 67 HA Group
1 " Centre Bde

SECRET

C/119/4

App. 78 /page 1/

ARTILLERY BARRAGE DURING RAID on HULLUCH SECTOR

101/2.5. Date to be notified later.

TIME	No. of Guns.	TARGET.	Rate of Fire.
			18-prs.
Zero to Zero +15.	6 18-prs.	H 25 D 73.09 to H 25 B 53.36 (Barrage on front line)	3 rounds per gun per minute.
	2 ,,	H 25 B 64.44 to H 25 B 86.56. (Enfilade Comm. trench).	
	8 ,,	H 25 B 41.37 to H 19 D 10.36. (Barrage on front line)	
			4.5" Hows.
	2 4.5" Hows.	H 25 B 62.44.	2 rounds per gun per minute.
	2 4.5" Hows.	H 25 B 32.54.	
	2 ,, ,,	H 19 D 35.24.	
	2 ,, ,,	H 19 D 47.30.	
	2 ,, ,,	H 19 D 00.54.	

TRENCH MORTARS

Zero to Zero + 20.	1 2" T.M.	H 25 D 35.45.	
	1 ,,	H 25 D 71.90.	
	1 ,,	H 25 B 52.38.	
	4 ,,	H 19 D 30.05 (Crater).	
		H 19 A 72.50 to H 13 C 55.32.	
	1 H.T.M.	H 31 B 15.75 (Dug-out).	
	1 ,,	H 25 B 90.60.	
	1 ,,	H 13 D 35.00.	
	1 H.T.M.	during afternoon previous to Raid to bombard Crater H 19 D 30.05.	

ACKNOWLEDGE.

27th Feby. 1917.

Brigade Major, 37th Divl. Artillery.

C/119/6.

SECRET

App 78
Page 2

I. Reference this office No. C/119/4 dated 27.2.17.
Trench Mortar Programme - bottom line - delete
"during afternoon previous to Raid".

II. The following additions are made to the Artillery
programme:-

2 18-prs. search H 25 D 28.28 to H 25 D 73.36   )
2 18-prs. search front line H 25 D 30.42 to H 25 D 71.82)
)
                                  3 rounds per gun per min)

HEAVY ARTY.

2 60-prs   search H 25 D 70.50 to)   1 round per
                  H 25 D 90.75.   )
1 6" How. H 25 D 67.48.   )   gun per minute.
1 6" How. H 25 D 90.50.   )

ACKNOWLEDGE.

                                           Major,
28.2.17.   Bde. Major, 37th Divl. Artillery.

TABLE "A"

Batteries, 37th Div.Arty.	Relieved by.		March To.
A/124 Bty. R.F.A.	21st Bty. R.F.A.)		
B/124 ,, ,,	42nd ,, ,,)	2nd Brigade, R.F.A.	BERGUETTE.
C/124 ,, ,,	53rd ,, ,,)		
D/124 ,, ,,	87th ,, ,,)		
A/123 Bty. R.F.A.	110th Bty. R.F.A.)		
B/123 ,, ,,	111th ,, ,,)	24th Brigade, R.F.A.	GUARBECQUE
C/123 ,, ,,	112th ,, ,,)		
D/123 ,, ,,	43rd ,, ,,)		
37th D.A.C.	6th D.A.C.		H.Q, & "A" Echelon - MOINGHEM. "B" ,, - GUARBECQUE.
37th D.T.M.	6th D.T.M.		MOINGHEM.

28.2.1917.

SECRET   Copy No. 15

37th DIVISIONAL ARTILLERY
OPERATION ORDER No. 47.

App. 79

1. The 37th Division will be relieved by the 6th Division in the LOOS, 14 BIS and HULLUCH Sections, between 1st and 5th March.

2. Infantry reliefs will be carried out as under:-

   LOOS and 14 BIS Section from LOOS CRASSIER)
   to GORDON ALLEY, H 31 C 2.0.   ) 16th Inf. Bde.

   GORDON ALLEY H 31 C 2.0 to BOYAU 70 . . . . 18th Inf. Bde.

   BOYAU 70 to BOYAU 77 . . . . 71st Inf. Bde.

3. The command of different Sections of the line will pass on completion of reliefs each day as under:-

   March 2nd. LOOS Section   - from 112th Inf. Bde. to
                                           16th Inf. Bde.
   March 3rd. 14 BIS Section -   ) From 63rd Inf. Bde.
               LOOS CRASSIER to GORDON ALLEY) to 16th Inf. Bde.

   March 3rd. 14 BIS Section -   ) From 63rd Inf. Bde. to
               GORDON ALLEY to BOYAU 63)   18th Inf. Bde.

   March 4th. HULLUCH Section -   ) From 111th Inf. Bde. to
               BOYAU 63 to BOYAU 70   )   18th Inf. Bde.

   March 4th. HULLUCH Section -   ) From 111th Inf. Bde. to
               BOYAU 70 to BOYAU 77   )   71st Inf. Bde.

4. The 37th Divl. Artillery will be relieved by the 6th Divl. Artillery on nights 4/5th and 5/6th and will move direct into the St. HILAIRE area under orders to be issued later.
   The 24th Brigade, RFA will relieve 123rd Bde. RFA and 2nd Brigade, RFA will relieve 124th Brigade, RFA.
   Incoming batteries will take over gun positions and wagon lines of opposite numbers in Brigades.
   The 37th Divl. Artillery will withdraw with guns complete.
   The 108th A.F.A. Brigade will remain in action covering the LOOS Section.
   The 37th Divl. Artillery will withdraw with 12 medium T.M's, handing over the 4 Heavy T.M's and surplus M.T.M's with Stores and indents for deficiencies.
   T.M. reliefs to be completed by 10 a.m. on 5th inst., relief being carried out under arrangements to be made by D.T.M.O's.
   The D.T.M.O., 6th Division will be at T.M.H.Q., 37th Division at 10 a.m. on March 2nd.

5.   The 6th Division front will extend from the DOUBLE CRASSIER to RAILWAY ALLEY G 4 A 70.95 and will be covered as follows:-

(a) From DOUBLE CRASSIER to GORDON ALLEY inclusive -
   covered by 108th A.F.A. Brigade and 1 Sect. 87th Batty.

(b) GORDON ALLEY exclusive to BOYAU 70 exclusive -
   covered by 2nd Bde. RFA less 1 Sect. 87th Batty.

(c) From BOYAU 70 inclusive to BOYAU 92 exclusive -
   covered by 24th Brigade, RFA.

(d) From BOYAU 92 inclusive to RAILWAY ALLEY covered by Infantry Brigade 21st Division and a group of 21st Div. Arty.

6.   At 12 noon on 3rd March the 108th A.F.A. Brigade will extend its present front to cover up to GORDON ALLEY (inclusive).
   124th Brigade, RFA will remain covering its present front up to 12 noon 4th March when it will cover from GORDON ALLEY (exclusive) to BOYAU 70 (exclusive).
   123rd Brigade, RFA will remain covering its present front up to 12 noon 4th March when it will cover from BOYAU 70 (inclusive) to BOYAU 92 (exclusive).

   The necessary registration etc. in connection with the above alterations in front to be carried out forthwith. (A further allotment of ammunition can be reckoned on to meet registration expenditure).

7.   The 37th D.A.C. will hand over to 6th D.A.C. on morning of March 5th at 12 noon, the 6th D.A.C. becoming responsible for the supply of ammunition from that time.
   Echelons will move full.

8.   Battery Commanders and two Officers per battery will visit Group H.Q. on 2nd March returning same day.
   Time of arrival will be notified and guides should be provided.

9.   Command of 37th Division area passes to G.O.C., 6th Division at 3 p.m. 4th March.
   Command of Artillery passes to C.R.A., 6th Division at 10 a.m. 6th March.

10.   Details of relief and ammunition arrangements will be issued later.

11.   ACKNOWLEDGE.

                                        Bacomhay
                                        Major,
27.2.1917.   Bde. Major, 37th Divl. Artillery.

Copy No.1   1st Corps, R.A.   No.7 21st Div. Arty.
     2   1st Corps, R.A.   8 6th Divisional Arty.
     3   1st Corps, R.A.   9 Right Group
     4   37th Division   10 Centre Group
     5   37th Division "Q"   11 Left Group
     6   2nd Can. Divn.   12 D.A.C.
                                     13 D.O.T.H.
                                     14 Staff Captain.
Amended 28/2/17   15 Diary

Please note the following amendments to 37th Divl. Artillery OPERATION ORDER No.47 dated 27.2.17 :-

Para.7.   For 11 a.m. read 12 NOON.

para.8.   For 1st March read 2nd March.

ACKNOWLEDGE.

28.2.17.

Major,
Bde.Major, 37th Divl. Artillery.

TABLE "A"

Batteries, 37th Div. Arty.	Relieved by.		March To.
A/124 Bty. R.F.A.	21st Bty. R.F.A.	⎫	
B/124	42nd ,,	⎬ 2nd Brigade, R.F.A.	BERGUETTE.
C/124	53rd ,,	⎭	
D/124	87th ,,		
A/123 Bty. R.F.A.	110th Bty. R.F.A.	⎫	
B/123	111th ,,	⎬ 24th Brigade, R.F.A.	GUARBECQUE
C/123	112th ,,	⎭	
D/123	43rd ,,		
37th D.A.C.	6th D.A.C.		H.Q. & "A" Echelon - MOINGHEM "B" ,, - GUARBECQUE.
37th D.T.M.	6th D.T.M.		MOLINGHEM.

28.2.1917.

App. 79

Reference 37th D.A. Operation Order No.48 para.viii.

The 37th D.A.C. will march to ST.HILAIRE area via
FOUQUEREUIL - CHOCQUES - BUSNES.

Batteries will march via BETHUNE and ROBECQ.

Acknowledge.

2.3.17.

Major,
Bde.Major, 37th Divl.Artillery.

MARCH TABLE.

Date	Formations in order of march.	From	To	Starting Point.	Time	Route	Remarks
March 9th	124th Bde.R.F.A. 123rd " 37th D.A.C.	BERGUETTE area.	ANVIN BERGUENEUSE HEUCHIN	X Roads ½ mile W of F in FANQUENHEM (1½ miles S of St.HILAIRE)	10.30 a.m.	AUCHY-au-BOIS WESTREHEM HEUCHIN	Order of march subject to alteration according to allotment of billets.
March 10th	124th Bde.R.F.A. 123rd Bde.R.F.A. 37th D.A.C.	ANVIN area.	St.MICHEL	X Roads 350x N of S in EPS	10.15 a.m.	EPS-HESTRUS- HUCLIER- BRYAS- OSTREVILLE.	Not to cross FERNES St.POL Road before 11.30 a.m.

NOTE. T.M.Batteries will march independently under orders of D.T.M.O. conforming to Route Orders.
Billets for 9th will be notified.

SECRET

Copy No 18

37th DIVISIONAL ARTILLERY

OPERATION ORDER No. 48.

App. 79

Ref: Hazebrouck
& Lens, 1/100,000.

I.   The relief of 37th Divisional Artillery by the 6th Divisional Artillery will be carried out on nights of 4/5th and 5/6th March in accordance with attached Table "A".

II.   Two sections per battery will be relieved first night- one section on second night of relief.
     Detached sections will be relieved first night. An Officer and two layers will be left by each detached section for 24 hours after completion of relief.
     All reliefs to take place after 6.30 p.m.

III.   On the morning of each day of relief, relieving batteries will take four or two guns, as the case may be, to the Wagon lines of batteries to be relieved. Staff Captain will make arrangements for accommodation.
     Relieving batteries will take guns into action with their own teams and will withdraw guns of 37th Div. Arty. to their respective Wagon lines, where battery teams will be hooked in.

IV.   One officer with telephonists from each H.Q. and battery of incoming Div. Arty. will be sent forward on 4th March to take over communications. Time of arrival will be notified and guides should be provided.

V.   H.Q. of Groups and batteries will hand over to corresponding formations all communications, maps, photographs, O.P's, Log-books, battery boards, alternative positions, Defence schemes and trench stores (gum boots, strombos horns, etc.), and all other information of value, obtaining receipts.

VI.   Batteries and D.A.C. 37th Division will march full with 75% A and 25% AX.
     All ammunition in gun positions and Wagon lines of batteries of 37th Div. Arty. will be handed over to incoming units at 12 Noon 5.3.1917.
     Batteries of 6th Divl. Artillery will hand over all ammunition in Wagon lines, filling up batteries of 37th Div. Arty. which they relieve.
     6th D.A.C. will take over all ammunition in 37th D.A.C.
     6th D.A.C. will hand over all ammunition which they bring into the new area, filling up the 37th D.A.C.
     Receipts for all ammunition to be given and taken, amounts being reported to Staff Captain by 8 p.m. on 6th March.
     Details of reliefs of D.A.C's to be arranged between D.A.C. Commanders concerned.

VII.   Staff Captain, 37th Divl. Artillery will meet representatives of units on 4th instant to arrange billets as under:-

     BERGUETTE   - 12 Noon.   )
     GUARBECQUE - 12.45 p.m.   )   At the Mairie in each case.
     MOLINGHEM   - 1.30 p.m.   )

VIII.   Relieved sections of batteries on each night will proceed as Brigades, direct to the new billetting area, under orders to be issued by Brigade Commanders.

Brigade Commanders and O.C. 37th D.A.C. will be responsible for making arrangements for traffic control when passing through large towns.

Distances of 200 yards to be maintained between Units

37th D.A.C. will march independently on completion of relief by 6th D.A.C., a distance of 200 Yards being maintained between every 18 vehicles.

Trench Mortar batteries will proceed direct to new billets by lorry on relief.

Route will be notified later.

IX.   All commands involved will pass on completion of relief.

X.   H.Q., 37th Div. Arty. will close at BRACQUEMONT at 10 a.m. 6th March and will re-open at 1 p.m. at BERGUETTE.

XI.   Completion of reliefs each night to be reported by code word "BOTTLE".

XII.   ACKNOWLEDGE.

Major,

Bde. Major, 37th Divl. Artillery.

1.3.17.

Copy No.		No.	
1	1st Corps, R.A.	10	Left Group
2	1st Corps, H.A.	11	D.O.T.M.
3	37th Division.	12	D.A.C.
4	37th Division "Q".	13	A.P.M.
5	6th Div. Arty.	14)	Divl.
6	21st Div. Arty.	15)	Train.
7	1st Canadian D.A.	16	Staff Captain
8	Right Group	17)	Diary.
9	Centre Group	18)	

SECRET   Copy No: 12

Ref.Map
LENS &
HAZEBROUCK
Sheets
1/100,000

37th DIVISIONAL ARTILLERY OPERATION
ORDER No: 4̶8̶ 49.

App. 80

I.   The 37th Divisional Artillery will march to ANVIN area on 9th instant, and to St MICHEL area on 10th instant as per attached March Table.

II. On 9th instant, the Staff Capt. will meet billeting parties (including H.Q.Coy.Divl.Train) at:-
     HEUCHIN (Mairie) ... 11.0 am.)
     BERGUENEUSE ,,   ... 11.30am.) (Allotment of billets
     ANVIN   ... ,,   ... 12 noon)   will be notified later)
On 10th instant the Staff Capt. will meet billeting parties (12 strong per battery & D.A.C.) at St MICHEL-Sur-TERNOISE at 10 am.

III. Brigade Commanders and O.C.D.A.C. to make the necessary arrangements for reconnoitring watering places, halts and traffic control. On 9th instant, Column to be clear of WESTREHEM before halting to water.

IV. The D.Arty. will move as a complete column, two hundred yards distance to be maintained between batteries and between groups of 18 vehicles D.A.C.

V.   On 10th inst. and subsequently, shrapnel helmets will be worn by all ranks.

VI. On arrival in new billets, location of H.Q. of Brigades and D.A.C. will invariably be notified to this office as soon as possible. H.Q. must be marked with flags or notice boards and luminous sign at night.

VII. Divisional Headquarters close at NORRENT FONTES at 12 noon 9th instant, re-opening at ROELLECOURT at same hour. Div.Arty.H.Q. close at BERGUETTE 8 a.m. 10th instant re-opening at St MICHEL at 10 a.m. same date.

VIII. Acknowledge.

Issued at noon
8th March/1917.

                                                    Major
                                 Brigade Major, 37th Divl.Artillery.

Copies to:-
    No:1 I Corps R.A.   6..123 Bde.R.F.A.   11..Staff Capt.
      2   VI Corps R.A.   7   124   12)
      3   37th Div.   8   37th D.A.C.   13) Diary.
      4   37th Div.Q.   9   D.O.T.M.
      5   A.P.M.   10   H.Q.Co.Train

Copy No. 16

37th Divisional Artillery

OPERATION ORDER No. 50.

App 81

Ref.
LENS
1/100,000

1. The 37th Divisional Artillery will move into the GROUCHES area (2½ miles N.E. DOULIENS) on 16th inst. coming under VII Corps from that date.

2. The Div. Arty. will march in two columns -
(a) 123rd & 124th Bdes. R.F.A. (in order of march)
(b) D.A.C.
   Starting point Column "A" Road junction 650 yds. West of S in St. MICHEL.
   Starting point Column "B" - Road junction immediately S of ROELLECOURT Church.
   Time in both cases at 7.30 a.m.

3. Column "A" will march via St.POL - HERLIN-le-SEC - HULCO - FREVENT - BOUQUEMAISON - Hte. VISEE.
   After passing HERLIN-le-SEC Brigades will march independently.

   Column "B" will march via: FOUFFLIN-RICAMETZ - TERNAS - HOUVIN-HOUVIGNEUL - ETREE-WAMIN - BEAUDRICOURT - LUCHEUX.

4. A distance of 500 yds. will be maintained between batteries - Also between Sections of the D.A.C.
   O's.C. Brigades and D.A.C. to make the necessary arrangements for traffic control when passing through towns.

5. Billeting parties will meet Staff Captain at Town Major's office GROUCHES at 12 Noon on 16th instant.

6. Attention is called to 37th D.A.O. No.1036 of 11.3.17.

7. H.Q., 37th Div. Arty. will close at St.MICHEL at 9 a.m. on 16th inst. and will reopen at COUTURELLE at 10.30 a.m.

8. ACKNOWLEDGE

15.3.1917.

Brigade Major, 37th Div. Arty.

Copy No.1 37th Division
      2 ,,   Q
      3 VI Corps, RA
      4 VII Corps RA
      5 A.P.M. 37th Divn.
      6 A.P.M. St.POL.
      7 A.P.M. Frevent.
      8 A.D.V.S.

No.9 123 Bde. RFA
10 124 ,,
11 37 D.A.C.
12 D.O.T.M.
13 Staff Capt.
14 H.Q.Coy.Train.
15 & 16 Diary.

NOTE:- Trench Mortars will proceed independently under D.T.M.O.
Bus arrangements will be notified.

App. 83

Copy No: 10

SECRET

37th DIVISIONAL ARTILLERY

OPERATION ORDER No. 52.

Ref: LENS
1/100,000.

Headquarters

1. The 124th Brigade, R.F.A., H.Q., A/124 and B/124 will march as soon as possible after receipt of this order, (under Brigade arrangements) to SIMENCOURT. These two batteries will go up into action tonight 21/22nd under orders which will be issued by 14th Div. Arty.
   22/23"

2. Route:- MILLY - LE MARAIS SEC - Main ARRAS Road - BEAUMETZ-LES-LOGES - SIMENCOURT.

3. Distance of 500 yds. to be maintained between batteries.

4. Billetting parties to meet Staff Captain, 14th Div. Arty. at Town Major's Office, SIMENCOURT at 3 p.m.

5. Time of starting to be notified by bearer to this office.

6. ACKNOWLEDGE.

Harcourt
Brigade Major,
37th Divisional Artillery.

21.3.1917.

Copy No. 1   37th Division.
         2   37th Divn. G.
         3   VII Corps R.A.
         4   123 Bde. RFA
         5   124   "
         6   37th D.A.C.
         7   D.O.T.M.
         8   H.Q. Coy. 37 Div. Train.
         9   Staff Captain.
    10 & 11 Diary.

SECRET   Copy No. 11

37th DIVISIONAL ARTILLERY

OPERATION ORDER No. 53.

App 84

Ref: LENS
1/100,000

1.   The 37th Divl. Artillery (including T.M.) will march on 23rd March from GROUCHES and LUCHEUX to SIMENCOURT.

2.   Starting point Road junction immediately N of C in L'ESPERANCE at 7 a.m.

3.   Route L'ESPERANCE - POMMERA - main ARRAS Road - BEAUMETZ-les-LOGES - SIMENCOURT.
        All vehicles etc. must be clear of POMMERA by 9 a.m.

4.   Distance of half a mile to be maintained between Batteries.

5.   Trench Mortars will march independently under D.O.T.M. Billetting arrangements and details of T.M. transport will be notified later.
        D.A.C. should be prepared to move on 23rd inst. at short notice.

6.   ACKNOWLEDGE.

                                            Brigade Major,
22.3.17.   37th Divl. Artillery.

No. 1   VII Corps, RA.
    2   Division
    3
    4   14th Div. Arty.
    5   123 Bde. RFA
    6   124   ,,
    7   37 D.A.C.
    8   D.O.T.M.
    9   No.1 Cpy. 37 Div. Train.
   10   Staff Captain.
11 & 12 Diary.

Vol 21 War Diaries
April 1917
57th Divl Arty.

Mar 1919

37 Div "Q"

I forward herewith War Diary of 37th Divisional Artillery for month of April 1917

2.5.17 Atkinson Lieut
for CRA 37 Div

WAR DIARY
or
INTELLIGENCE SUMMARY.
(Erase heading not required.)

Army Form C. 2118.

Place	Date	Hour	Summary of Events and Information	Remarks and references to Appendices
April 1917.				
	9.		2/Lt G.M. St Ledger wounded by shrapnell.	
	12.		37 D.A. personnel exchanged positions & guns with 50th D.A. in forward positions under orders of 14th D.A.	Appx App/10
	13.		37 D.A. moved with late 50th Divisional guns complete to 21st D.A.	Appx App/11
			21 D.A. going into action N.W. of CROISILLES, wagon lines at BUISLIEUX St MARC & BOYELLES	
	14		Div Arty H.Q. moved to BUISLIEUX au MONT C.R.A. & command 37th D.A. but under CRA & 21st Div. 155 Army Field Arty Bde attached to 37 D.A.	
	16		37 D.A H.Q. moved to HAMLINCOURT, Bdes 123 & 124 moved sections & all Batteries up to St MARTIN sur COJEUL, D Bde to BOIRY BECTRUDE/17th C/123 had one gun condemned by 10 am 7th Corps.	Appx App/12
	17		Remaining sections moved up to St MARTIN. Bde H.Qrs moved 123 B/de to BOIRY RECQUÉRELLE, H.Q.P. 124 Bde H.Q. to HENIN SUR COJEUL. 155 AFA Bde ordered to withdraw Range for lines.	Appx App/3
	18		155 AFA Bde ordered to join VI Corps ceased to be attached 37 D.A. Bombardments carried out according to allotted tasks searching roads & tracks. e.T.G. etc at night, wiping out mark by day	

WAR DIARY
or
INTELLIGENCE SUMMARY.

(Erase heading not required.)

Army Form C. 2118.

Place	Date	Hour	Summary of Events and Information	Remarks and references to Appendices
April	18		S.O.S. was signalled on night at about 9.45 pm & answered. Position with our infantry not being clear a slow barrage was opened on S.O.S. line until about 10.15 pm when Inf. reported all quiet. S.O.S. was ascertained to be alarm apparently sent up by enemy.	
April	21		Batteries of both Bdes. with exception of C/129 moved into open country owing to enemy shelling.	App App/4
	22		Lt. C.S. Heape wounded slightly. Shrapnel. Bdes carried out bombardment during day and harassing shoots about 7.35 pm and changed to hostile from about 11.45 pm & 1.0 am.	App App/5
	23		2Lt. C.W. Shilcock wounded seriously by [?] premature. 37 D.A. took part in attack on Hindenburg Line etc. see Appendix. Zero hour 4.45 a.m. Infantry driven back as listed in App. New attack on Army front zero hour 6 pm.	App App/6 Operations Report
	24		Enemy retiring from Hindenburg Line. No[?] River C/123 & B/124 moved to T5c 2.5 + T3b 0.5	App App/7
	25		Enemy retired to high ground still holding Hindenburg line South of road U.1.c. [?] to NE along road. See artillery map. Reconnaissance - 33 Div lies at [?] Shores by 21 Div. 25/26 [?]	
	26		1 gun of B/123 moved to N.35.d.4.0. HQ/125 Bde moved to T.10.a.00 C.O.C. 21 Div took over line.	
	27		1 How of D/123. - N.2.a.c.6.4. Bombardment in support of Inf. attack to take Hindenburg [?] [App App/?] Line down river. Attack took place 3. a.m. 28th & failed	

WAR DIARY
or
INTELLIGENCE SUMMARY.

(Erase heading not required.)

Army Form C. 2118.

Place	Date	Hour	Summary of Events and Information	Remarks and references to Appendices
1917 April	28th		Barrage fire as above. 1 Section A/123 moved to T.4.b.7.2. and remaining batteries D/123 moved to N.29.c.c.4.	
	29th		B/123 moved to N.35.d.a.7.9.	
	30		B/123 moved to T.7.b.1.9. Escape hanger took place from 5.45 am. see Operation Report. App. 6.	

C. Newman Major RA
for Brigade Major RA
37 Div. Arty.

App. Apr/6 Page 1

OPERATION REPORTS.

Date.	Time.	From.	Report.	Action.
23.4.17.	Message 10 Rec'd [?]	124 Bde	Message timed 5.25 am. Enemy putting up fairly strong barrage in N 35 c and a. Message timed 5.40. Barrage on support trenches was decreasing. Machine gun fire can be heard in direction of N 26 D. Progress appears satisfactory, but mist & smoke make observation difficult.	Repeated to 21st DA over phone.
	M/A 18 Sent 6.5 am Rec'd 6.11 am	124 Bde	Bde Liaison Officer reports at 5.58 a.m. left brigade are in touch with division on left. They have taken 35 prisoners of 61st Regt.	
	Y 33 Rec'd 6.12 am	123 Bde	Right reports that temporarily held up. First objective gained.	
	Y 34 Rec'd 6.17 am	123 Bde	Liaison Officer reports 67 prisoners have come in. A further batch of 61 prisoners report from liaison Officer at right battalion.	
	M/A 20 Sent 6.10 Rec'd 6.25.	124 Bde	Right F.O.O. reports 6 am. Enemy was very clear golden rain + red rockets sent up within one minute of zero. Barrage on support line mostly 7.7 m.m. and 4.2 6 m gm. Considerable machine gun fire from the two direction of FONTAINE. Mist + smoke preclude observation of Progress. 5.35 am. Tanks are at U 1 c 2 0.	
	M/A 21 Rec'd 6.28 am.	124 Bde	Left F.O.O. reports at 6.15 am. that on objective (1st) was gained immediately after Barrage lifted. It appears that over 100	

Page 2.

OPERATION REPORTS.

Date.	Time.	From.	Report.	Action.
23.4.17	M/A 21 Rec'd 6.28 am continued	124 Bde.	over one hundred, prisoners have already been brought in on our immediate front.	
	M/A 23 Rec'd 7.15 am M/A 23	124 Bde	Order from Football (14 Div'l Division) 6.45 am reads. Please barrage N36 c 65.70 to N36 c 70.60. Then creep forward to next objective. Such Order passed to OATCRENE (123 Bde) altered 37 D.A. + 123.	(a) These orders altered verbally by Liaison Officer about 4.12.3. Co-ords were altered to N36 c 5.5 N36 c 6.6. Standard barrage till orders. Arty co-ord to be as above. Greyjoint
	M A 22 Rec'd 7.25 a.p.	124.	It appears that an infantry gained Hindenburg line up to 41 c 05. An aeroplane has come down in T.A.A. The machine made a good landing. It is numbered B.E 2 C. F.O.O. at T 6 a. 0.3. repeats 6.26 am. Pilot & observer officers good. Our rep reports by wounded to be near Bourn & river. Consid. Machine gun fire from FONTAINE. Enemy rapidly reed own plane & dealth with. See above (a).	
	M A 24 Rec'd 7.28 am	124	Rep my M A 23 barrage began from 7.10 to 7.15 am Inf. set to creep forward. Addressed 37 D.A. + 123 Bde	
	Verbal message 7.30 am	124.	Enemy Inf seen at {N 36 a 3.7.6 {moving N.W. suspected to {N 36 a 3.7.5 } be reinforcements.	
	Verbal message 7.31 am	124	Enemy Inf. disappeared action suspended	

Page 3.

OPERATION REPORTS.

Date.	Time.	From. Bde. RFA	Report.	Action.
23.4.17	Message M426 Recd 8.6 a.m.	124	Message from J.O.O. timed 7.23 a.m. reads. Enemy infantry on the ridge N36 a 7.6. to N36 d 30.7.5. They appeared to be moving in N.W. direction. Message timed 7.28 a.m. reads prisoners now passed O.P. over 420. Hostile Infantry reported in last message have now disappeared.	
	Recd M427 8.12 a.m.	124	F.O.O. report Timed 7.30 reads. Red lights were seen + we opened fire on S.O.S. lines and we are still firing. Right F.O.O. repeats. At 7.30 a.m. white very lights seen from V.16.2. We can see some of our infantry in V.I.C.	
	Recd M428 8.17 a.m.	124	Bde L.O.H. reports. On left Suffolks got down to within 200 yds of river. Later Germans reported holding out in W.of copse in N 36 c and barrage by 123 Bde was turned on. Nothing heard since then, but we held T.6.b.5.7.	
	Recd M429 8.23 a.m.	124	J.O.O. report recd 8.3 a.m. reads. An m Machine Gun emplacement T 6 d.0.6. which was holding us up, and Rvrs just been rushed at 7.40 a.m. Advance is held up by a stronghold at T.6.d.4.4. Stokes guns are just about to shape this point. From T6d 0.6. On left the advance appeared to have been carried further. Tank has just arrived to assist in taking stronghold at T6d 4.4.	
	Verbal message 8.20 a.m.	124	Bosche ran South to T6 d.4.4. Very light seen at T.12 b.8.4.	
	Verbal through HQ 8.45 a.m.	123	F.O.O. reports that our infantry are in FONTAINE Wood.	

Page 4.

OPERATION REPORTS.

Date.	Time.	From.	Report.	Action.
23.4.17	Monday M.4.30. Rec'd 8.57 pm	124	Highest finish 8.45am. 7th Liaison Off. Suffolks report on right are digging in on final objective and are in touch with Argylls in centre, who are also digging in on final objective. Argylls are in touch with middle & those left is uncertain. No news of division on right.	
	Verbal 10.20am	21 D.A	A line of enemy seen in O.34 central and 50 following 123 & 124 Bdes. moving towards FONTAINE, in O.35 & O.36. moving towards FONTAINE. reserved.	
	Verbal 10.0 am	123	200 enemy infantry seen at 10.30 going from FONTAINE due east to Copse in U.5 a and b. – Tank observed in U.16 going S.E. along Hindenburg line	
	Verbal 11.12 am	124	Reported large body of enemy 200, & 300 strong seen moving from O.33 & O.34	Passed to 21 D.A. Heavies only informed by them.
	Verbal 11.38 am	123	F.O.O. reported our right fallen back up HINDENBURG Line behind road T.6 d 7.4.	21 D.A. no action by us needed already dealt with by H.A.
	Verbal 11.47 am	124	Large bodies of enemy seen moving towards our infantry, hun dictator N.W. of FONTAINE Wood.	124 Bde fired on with one Battery, 123 Bde. also one Battery.
	Verbal 12.35 pm	21st D.A	33rd Div. now make situation to be, our infantry in places back in front line. Some still in front line of Hindenburg come down N.36 and heavy bombing in progress. Some of our infantry probably still out beyond. Our batteries are to be ready to turn on a Swiss on original open barrage, keeping clear of Hindenburg line from East of Swiss Cottage. 123 Bde Howitzers not to fire unless specially ordered. No other further be done however unless fuhin orders are received. Enemy seen to be digging in on final objective east of Hindenburg line.	

Page 5

OPERATION REPORTS.

Date.	Time. Recd.	No.	From.	Report.	Action.
23.4.17	Verbal 12.55pm	Recd	123	F.O.O. observed at 12.43 pm about 1000 enemy in U16.b. Large amount Troops & Transport on road O33d, O33rd, O9b, moving in both directions.	Passed to 21 D.A.
	Verbal 1X.25pm		21.D.A.	We hold whole of front line of HINDENBURG down to river. Trench junction at T6.b.6.7. reported to be blocked.	123 Bde ordered to put How Btty. on trench junction, trench junction to main trail. Small Howitzer will pour action.
	Verbal .27pm		124	Considerable number of enemy advancing in open front above 1.10 pm. Westel.	
	1.27pm		12A	Very large body of enemy observed in O33d over 1000 strong. About destroyed by our 18 pdr fire.	
	Verbal 2.15pm		21.D.A.	A counter attack has taken place in U7a and we have lost portion of HINDENBURG front line South of river.	
	AL32 Aurge. no time recd 2.27pm		124	F.O.O. reports Enemy hold HINDENBURG line as far as T6.a 0-8. 2.0pm heavy bombing is going on at this point where he is attempting to enter red front line along trench T6 a S.2.	
	F3 Aurge. 3.15pm recd 3.0pm		124	Am. F.O.O. reports our infantry have been seen returning from FONTAINE-les-CROISSILLES going S.W. They were seen about T12c.	

Page. 6.

OPERATION REPORTS.

Date.	Time. No.	Time Recd.	From.	Report.	Actn.
	C040	4·10pm	124 3·55pm	Bn.F.O.O. reports enemy hold HINDENBURG line as far as T6a 0-8. They are still trying to enter the red line along trench at T6a 8·0 and also along trench T6a 1-5 but have not yet succeeded. Bombing has continued at the point of contact for the last hour. T5b backward line with 105 & 150mm. Situation in U7 is not clear.	
	DR14	4·47pm	124	F.O.O. reports our infantry falling back from #3 U1c. Enemy have effected an entry in to front line in T6d1-6.	
	C141	4·57pm	124	Cutting off the SAPPERS. Rear machine a barricade at T6a 6-1. Enemy is attempting to enter at T6a 2.3. Shoe bomb fighting is going on.	

OPERATION REPORTS.

Page. 7

Date	Time Recd.	No.	From	Report	Action
23.4.17	21st D.A. Operation order Recd noon 5.10 pm			Ordering original barrage lines of this morning to be again fired at 6.0pm + same line, attack to take place on whole 3rd Army front.	Orders retransmitted to Bdes + Barrage opened punctually.
	Verbal 7.25pm		21st D.A.	Order from General Wellesley to 'Stop Barrage at 7.30pm'	carried through out.
	7.52pm 3rd 9.7.30		124 Bde	Liaison Officer reports the attack has failed will you get through to Division and ask whether we can stop the barrage as infantry have not moved at all. S.O.S. repeated at T6a.13. + T6	Already stopped (above)
	Verbal 9.0pm		123 Bde		
	9.10pm	—	21 D.A.	Order howitzer battery on T6A.13. and T6a.1.8. Enemy reported to be bombing up into Hindenburg front line.	D/123
	9.38pm	—	to 123.	Liaison Officer ask 124 to put S.O.S on front barrage this morning 3rd Inf Liaison Officer asked to put a stop after 10 minutes. To put up Howitzer barrage. Enemy suspected of trying to bomb up to Hill 105, 75A	123 to get on to 124 + find out whether. Bde asked to put up barrage at once.
	9.40	—	: 123 : 124.		
	10.10	—	124	Liaison officer states that infantry say they are alright + do not wish 18pdr barrage unless asked for.	
	10.27	—	124	State of infantry is exactly as it was when we began this morning on Bde front. Not known what is happening to bombing up + but bears expected.	
	Verbal 10.50		124	Liaison Officer reports that Inf Bde is in touch with flanks right + left. Bde H.Q. is in touch with flanks Bde HQs with wireless + visual. They are getting into communication with them + enquiring whether flanks are still in touch with one another.	

OPERATION REPORTS.

Date.	Time. Recd.	No.	From.	Report.	Action.
23.4.17	11.12pm	V63pA	21.DA.	Old block at T5b84 to T5b88 said to have been recaptured by us.	
	11.16pm	—	37DA to 124Bde	Ask Liaison Officer whether infantry require on Howitzer fire in T6a 1.3. + T6a 8.3. to continue. Infantry state that their left flank is in the air but right is in touch by means of by posts with left of Bde on right.	
	12.15pm	—	21.DA.	Night shelling of communication trenches, roads, and Zonnebeke to be carried out during the night.	Zonnebeke 6 123 v 134.
24.4.17	9.0am	B.M. 179	21.I.A.	Enemy are retiring and our infantry occupy yesterday's first objective in N36. Patrols are being pushed out from there, and down the HINDENBURG line. Warm F.O.O. to keep touch and report on our line.	
	9.7am	M437	124Bde.	Liaison officer reports. We have taken just beyond the of yesterday and are pushing on to final objective. S.O.S lines with Hunfire be adjusted to those now in crack. Moved for yesterday evening i.e. D31 c 8.6 to U1a 2-1 to U1d 3.5 addressed all Batteries - repeated ONTINE (37 JA) and 123 Bde	
	9.30pm	R39	21.I.A.	Enemy reported to have retired about left Brigade of 33 Divn which has advanced approximately to blue line N of HINDENBURG line and patrols are pushing on.	

Page 9.

OPERATION REPORTS.

Report.

Date.	Time. Rec'd.	No.	From.	Report.	Action.
2.4.17	9.10am	Verbal	B.M. to 123 & 124	Orders issued to 123 Bde to push forward C Battery to a position west of ridge somewhere about T.4.	
	12.5pm	M439	124	Liaison Officer reports at 11.30 am we are now at sunken road U.1.C.40 to U.1.d.6.8. There is a good deal of sniping going on.	
	1.25pm	M441	124	Bde Liaison Officer reports that the enemy were in Hindenburg trench at 10 am but at some time after this they left, apparently in great haste as they have left numbers of rifles and equipment. Following repts from F.O.O. rec'd 12.35 pm. (1) About six explosions have been seen in HÉNINCOURT and RÉINCOURT. The enemy appear to be demolishing these villages. Otherwise everything quiet. (2) One or two of our infantry have been seen walking in FONTAINE wood. Information given to Bde liaison Officer in M.44'.	
	1.10pm	M440	124		
	1.40pm	M442	124	was obtained from two prisoners.	
	1.50pm	G.B.107	123	C Battery 123 is in action at T.5.c.2.5.	
	2.15pm	Verbal	to 124	C Battery 124 to move to about T.4.b.0.5. at once.	
	2pm	BM189	2.1.D.M	Enemy has apparently retired to high ground S. of river Sensée. Division will consolidate as follows FROGAL HINDENBORG support line & ptive up to Army boundary. If enemy has retired that line FOOTBALL (ex Puppem) HINDENBORG support line N of river Sensée to T.G. & thence to road junction in O.31.C. Patrols will be pushed forward by FROGAL as far S.E. edge of FONTAINE and sunken road U.8.a.d.c. By FOOTBALL a puppem as far as Sensée river in first place secondly into FONTAINE.	

Page. 10.

OPERATION REPORTS.

Date.	No.	Time Recd.	From Bde.	Report.	Action.
24.4.17	A/31	4.30pm	124	F.O.O. Reports the enemy can be seen retiring in extended order from the HINDENBURG LINE to U13b and U14c going towards wood in U12a very heavy barrage on the left of our zone on HINDENBURG Line. C/124 in action at T4b0.6.	
	Verbal M/445	7.6pm	124	At O.29.c.1.9. seven men were seen starting out a trench at 6.45pm.	
	M/446	7.46pm	124	Liaison Officer reports from N36 a.3.2. to HINDENBURG LINE T6A5.6. and continuing eastwards N36.c.7.3. to HINDENBURG LINE T6A5.6 and continuing eastwards for about 300 yds from copse a few enemy snipers are still this side of the river pontaine of Germans can continually be seen in FONTAINE and FONTAINE Wood.	
25.4.17	SP3	8.45pm	123	Between B45 and 4.45 am our Artillery put up a heavy barrage on left about GUÉMAPPE to which hostile Artillery replied all along line. Night calm.	
	M452	10.25ah	124	Bde Liaison Officer reports at 10.25 am our patrols did not enter FONTAINE wood and village. They are at present home open troops in there places. The enemy still holds a strong point N.W. of river.	
	21DA 0p.0.51	12.30pm	21DA	33 Div (less Arty) to be relieved by 21 Div (less Arty) by 3 a.m. 26th April. heavy	
	M461	6.30pm	124	F.O.O. reports enemy putting up barrage on his own front line T6B5T6a2d also spray rockets can be seen going up from FONTAINE. Enemy barraged his own lines in O7 about and a number of enemy were killed by their own fire. Large masses of enemy were seen across the open. Big explosion was heard at 6.40pm	App Apr/S.a.

Page 11.

OPERATION REPORTS.

Date	Time	No.	Recd. From	Report	Action
25.4.17	Verbal 8.40pm		129	F.O.O. reports much movement on roads north west of Fontaine and suggests a relief taking place.	123 ?Ordered to 124 Shell C.T. Roads and Tracks.
	BM/194 4.0pm		21 DA	Prisoner 237 R.I.R. captured this morning S. of Coseul about O.20 states 199 Div consisting of 237 R.I.R and 257 R I R is relieving 18 B.av. and 141 I.R. to-night. Prisoners of 176 I.R. captured S.W. of CHERISY yesterday say N.C.O. and 4 men of 119 G.R 26 Div arrived to see line prior to taking over.	
26.4.17	Verbal			Headquarters 123 Bde moved to T.10.c.0.0. 1 Gun B/123 moved N.35 d 40.	
27th	0.051	25th	21 DA	33 Div. heavy Artillery relieved by 21 Div. heavy sea Artillery	
	G.B.131	8 pm	123 Bde	1 How D/123 in action N.29 c 0.4.	
	G.B.128	4.15 pm		1 Gun B/123 in action N.35 d 30	
28th	23	8.10	123	Up to 3 am enemy were quiet. At 3 a.m. on bombing parties started. 3.55 a.m information was received that the party in Hindenburg front line had reached their objective and were rapidly consolidating. The parties in support line met with strenuous opposition + heavy fighting ensued and is continuing. The position of parties now are U1C.40.00 + U1C.40.4ᵃ. The enemy put up no barrage until 3.28 a.m and then it was neither strong or effective. Our barrage was reported good & effective. At 4.20 am enemy reopened his barrage which was heavy + lasted an hour, but did no serious damage. At present Hostile Artillery is quiet. Casualties light. Remaining howitzer D/123 now in action N.29 c 0.4.	
	G.B.142	11 am	123		
	G.B.146	6.55 pm	123	1 Section A/123 now in action registered at T.A.b 7.2.	

Page 12.

OPERATION REPORTS.

Date.	Time Recd.	No.	From.	Report.	Action.
24th	8.21am	T1	123.	Enemy have attacked with bombing party up HINDENBURG support trench we have been driven back about 30 yards.	
	5.22pm	M/301	124	One section of B/battalion moved to T4 & 6.7.	
30th		Artillery Surgeon	paris	Copt. Damage took three prisoners at 4.5am. Before 4 am there was a steady shelling of 5.9" along HINDENBURG LINE in front of L.H.R. Enemy barrage opened this caused a number of A.2 casualties fell on + behind	

app. Apr/7

SECRET.   Map Ref.   C/153/11
          BULLECOURT. 1/10,000

1.   Reference 64th Infantry Brigade Operation Order
          No:116.

2.   The barrage will be formed by the 37th Divisional
          Artillery and 94th Brigade, R.F.A.

3.   Tasks:-
   94th Bde.R.F.A.
          4 18 prs.   U 1 C 70.75 - U 1 B 70.10 enfilade.
          4 18 prs.   U 1 D 12.45 - U 1 D 75.95 enfilade.
          2 Hows.   U 1 C 70.76
          2 Hows.   U 1 D 12.47
          2 18 prs.) Comm.Tr. ... U 7 A 65.70 - U 7 B 04.90
          2 Hows.) (Hows.on Junction points; 18 prs.searching.
          2 18 prs.   searching U 7 A 65.70 - U 7 B 04.90
                                U 7 A 75.53 - U 7 B 12.71

   123rd Bde.R.F.A.
          4 18 prs. searching U 1 D 38.10 - U 7 B 04.90
                              U 7 B 12.71 - U 7 B 48.95.
          (C/12 3 is not to fire.)

   124th Bde.RFA.
          2 18 pr.Batteries searching U 1 A 40.00 - U 1 D 12.45
          U 7 B 48.95 - U 2 C 00.60 - U 1 B 70.10
          1 How.   U 2 C 0.6
          1 How.   U 1 D 75.95
          2 18 prs.   U 2 C 00.60 - U 1 B 70.10
          4 Hows.)
          4 18 prs.) Searching wood in U 2 A.

4.   Rate of fire:- 2 rounds per gun & how per minute.

5.   Watches will be synchronised with Artillery Liaison
          Officer with 9th K.O.Y.L.I. at 2 a.m. and 2.30 a.m. 28th inst.
                Brigades to make arrangements for keeping in immed-
          iate touch with liaison officer.
                Liaison officer will notify when fire is to be dis-
          continued.

6.   Acknowledge.

Issued at 8 p.m.   Major
27.4.1917.
                        Brigade Major, 37th Divl.Artillery.

        Copies to:-   21st Div.   21st Div.Arty.
                      64 Inf.Bde. Liaison Officer
                      123 Bde.R.F.A. 124 Bde.R.F.A.

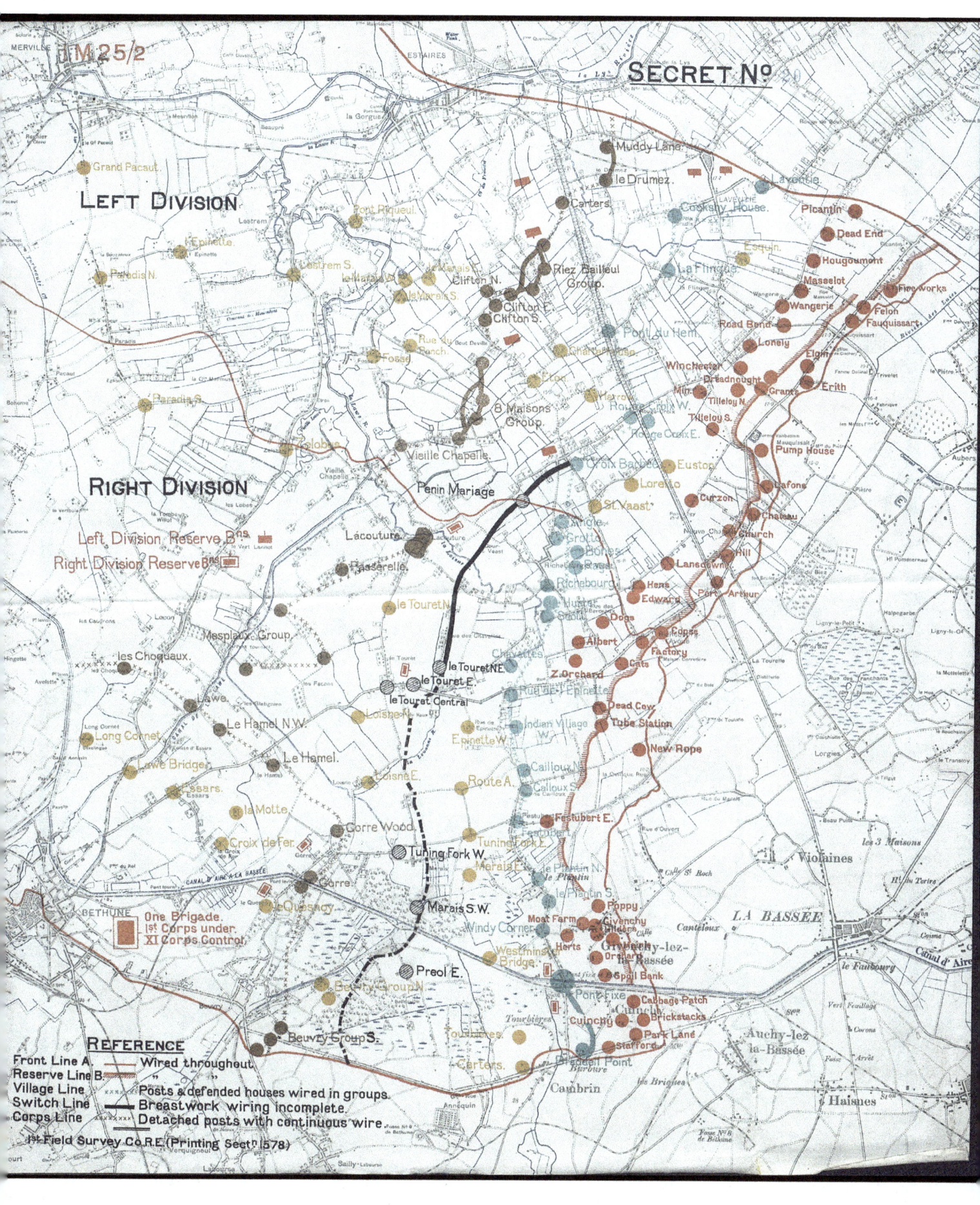

App. April

S E C R E T.   37th Divisional Artillery   G.121/9.

Operation Order No.57.

App. April/3

(1)   The 155th A.F.A.Brigade will be withdrawn from action night 17th/18th under orders to be issued later.

(2)   This office No.G/121/6 is cancelled with exception of para.6.

(3)   From 7 p.m. 17th inst., 123rd Brigade R.F.A. will cover Right Battalion, and 124th Brigade R.F.A. the Left Battalion 98th Infantry Brigade.

(4)   Liaison officer with Infantry Brigade H.Q. will be found by 124th Brigade R.F.A. relief to take place by 7 p.m. 17th inst.

(5)   Acknowledge.

17.4.17.   Major,
                                    Bde.Major, 37th Div. Arty.

SECRET

App. Apr/1   No. 12

37th DIVISIONAL ARTILLERY OPERATION ORDER No.54.

Ref:
51b SW.
Ed.4a. 1/20,000.

1. The 37th Divl. Artillery will move complete from 50th Div. Arty. positions into the 21st Divisional area as soon as possible after 5 p.m. to-day.

2. The 123rd Brigade, RFA will take over positions as soon as vacated by opposite numbers of 290th F.A.Brigade, becoming "Left sub-Group". 124th Brigade, RFA will take over positions as soon as vacated by opposite numbers of 291st F.A.Brigade, becoming "Right sub-group".
  Battery representatives should be sent on to reconnoitre battery positions as soon as convenient.
  Right Group H.Q., Col. Fitzgerald, A 4 D 9.3.
  Left Group H.Q., Col. Odam, S 18 A 2.8.

  Right Sub-Group H.Q. (291st Brigade, RFA) T 25 A 7.3.
     B/291   T 27 C 7.7.
     C/291   T 28 A 0.3.
     D/291   T 28 C 45.90.

  Left Sub-Group H.Q. (290th Bde. RFA) S 14 C 4.5.
     A/290   S 6 B 09.85.
     B/290   M 36 D 10.10.
     C/290   T 13 C 30.40.
     D/290   S 11 C 55.75.
     A/291   T 7 A 30.10.

  A/124 will probably move into a position under Right Sub-Group, but position has not yet been decided.

3. ROUTE via BEAURAINS - MERCATEL - BOYELLES Road under Brigade arrangements.
  This road needs to be reconnoitred.

4. 37th D.A.C. will move as soon as possible after receipt of these orders to a position to be selected about S 20 A 3.8.
  An Officer should be sent on at once to reconnoitre for a suitable position.

5. Echelons will move full.
  Ammunition will be drawn from ADINFER DUMP.
  Ammunition on positions to be counted and amount found reported to Staff Captain, 21st Divl. Artillery as soon as possible.

6. H.Q.Coy. Train will move on 13th inst. at 3 a.m. to position vacated by 58th Div. Train on ADINFER - DOUCHY Road.

7. Communications will be taken over by Brigade Orderly Officers forthwith.

8. One mounted Orderly per Brigade to be sent forthwith to 21st D.A.H.Q. (X 26 A 4.4, Sheet 51c S.E. 1/20,000).

9. Movement of 37th D.A.H.Q. will be notified.

10. Completion of move to be notified to 21st D.A.H.Q.

11. ACKNOWLEDGE.

                                                            Major, R.A.
                              Brigade Major, 37th Divl. Artillery.

12.4.1917.

Issued at 2.30 p.m.

Copies to-
No.1 123 Bde. RFA
   2 124   ,,
   3 37th Divn. A.
   4 37th Divn. G.
   5 14th Div. Arty.
   6 21st   ,,
   7 VII Corps, R.A.
   8 37th D.A.C.
   9 D.T.M.O.
  10 S.C.
  11 A.D.V.S. 37 Div.
  12 & 13 Diary.
  14 VII Corps H.A.
  15 HQ Co. 37 D. Train

App. Ap/O

3/CRA/18/91
12-4-17.

1. 50th D.A. (personnel only) and 37th D.A. (personnel only) will relieve each other in action on April 12th in accordance with 14th D.A. Operation Order No. 83 attached.

2. (a) The advance parties of each Brigade Headquarters and Battery of 50th D.A. will report to corresponding Brigade Headquarters and Battery of 37th D.A. at 10 a.m. on morning of 12th.

   (b) The remaining personnel of 50th D.A. Batteries will leave present positions at 12 NOON on 12th instant at which time they will come under the orders of C.R.A. of 14th Division.

3. On relief a statement of ammunition in possession of 50th D.A. Batteries will be rendered to 56th D.A. showing amount of each nature

   (a) At present positions.

   (b) Remaining in positions ~~previously located~~. Vacated

   (c) In Echelons.

4. All telephone systems, less telephones belonging to units, will be handed over in situ.

5. 37th D.A. on taking over from 50th D.A. will proceed to 21st Division under orders received from C.R.A., 21st Division.

Major,
Brigade Major, R.A.,
56th Division.

12-4-17.

Copies to:-

50th D.A.
250th Bde. R.F.A.
251st Bde., R.F.A.
14th D.A.
37th D.A.
123rd Bde, R.F.A.
124th Bde., R.F.A.
56th Div.
WAR DIARY.

Secret.

Ref.Map
51b S.W.
1/20,000

Diary App. App 2
Copy No:

37th Divisional Artillery Operation
Order No: 56

1. C/123 Bde.R.F.A. will move a Section night 16/17th to a position from which the HINDENBURG support line in T 6 A and T 6 B can be enfiladed.
    Remaining Sections will move night 17/18th.
    D/123 Bde.R.F.A. will move to a position near that selected for C/123 from which it can enfilade the HINDENBURG line in T 6. One Section should move into the new position if possible during night 16/17th remaining Sections night 17/18th.

2. B/123 & C/123 (available guns) will carry out enfilade fire on the HINDENBURG line with ammunition as allotted in 37th Div.Arty.Operation Order 55 commencing as soon as possible after midnight 16/17th
    D/123 to co-operate as soon as any guns have been moved into new position.

3. 124th Bde.R.F.A. will move at earliest opportunity - (if possible first sections night 16/17th - remainder night 17/18th) to positions S.W. of HENINEL from which to deal with Northern frontage & zone as detailed for 123rd Bde. in 37th Div.Arty.Operation Order No:55.

4. Completion of all moves to be reported by wire to this office.

5. On completion of (which will be notified from this office) move of 124th Brigade frontages and zones will be reallotted as follows:-
    124th Bde.R.F.A. ... ... Northern zone.
    123rd Bde.R.F.A. ... ... Centre zone.
    155th Army Fd.Arty.Bde. ... Southern zone.

6. As soon as 124th Bde. has moved into new position it will find liaison officer with Left battalion and 123rd Bde. will find liaison officer with Right battalion.

7. 155th A.F.A.Bde. will reconnoitre positions between 123rd & 124th Bde.R.F.A. suitable for barraging centre or Southern zone. Report on proposed positions to be sent in to this office by 10 a.m. on 17th instant.

8. The above movements have reference to a probable attack and advance in a S.E. direction, details of which will follow.

9. Acknowledge.

Issued at 8 p.m.
16/4/1917.

Major
Brigade Major, 37th Divl.Artillery.

Copies to 123 Bde.R.F.A.   30 Div.Arty.
         124 Bde.R.F.A.   War Diary.
         37th D.A.C.
         33rd Division

Appendix Ap/1
33 GS B1.

SECRET

33 Div. G.S. Ins. B.1.
COMMUNICATIONS AND LIAISON.

1. During the forthcoming operations Div. H.Q. will remain at RAMELINCOURT. A Report Centre will, however, be established at the Div. O.P. where messages can be handed in for transmission to Div. H.Q.

2. Bde. H.Q. will be established as follows :-

    100 Inf. Bde. Adv. H.Q.   Near Div. O.P.

    98 Inf. Bde. Adv. H.Q.   In HINDENBURG Line in T.3.

    19 Inf. Bde.   ...   In T.3.

3. Inf. Bdes. will arrange for Liaison Officers as follows :-

    19 Inf. Bde.   At Div. H.Q.

    98 Inf. Bde.   With 90 Inf. Bde.

    100 Inf. Bde.   With 98 Inf. Bde.

    91 Inf. Bde. will probably send Liaison Officer to 100 Inf. Bde.

4. ARTILLERY ARRANGEMENTS :-

    100 Inf. Bde.   supported by -

        21 Div. Art. and 150 Army F.A.Bde. Detachment 62 Div. Art.

        Art. Liaison Officer of 21 Div. Art. at Inf. Bde. H.Q.

    98 Inf. Bde.   supported by -

        37 Div. Art.

        Art. Liaison Officer at Inf. Bde. H.Q.

    Each F.A. Bde. is in direct communication with those on either flank.
    There will be direct communication with heavy Artillery H.Q. from Div. H.Q.
    Liaison Officers of Heavy Artillery will be with Inf. Bdes. and will be in telephonic communication with their own Groups.

5. Wireless Sets will be in position as follows :-

    One at 98 Inf. Bde. Adv. H.Q.

    One in vicinity of Div. O.P. and 100 Inf. Bde. Adv. H.Q.

6. Following rules will be observed regarding the use of tunnel under the HINDENBURG Support Line :-

    Only parties going up to the front, i.e., moving West to East, may proceed along the tunnel, with the exception of runners and signallers, who may proceed in either direction. 98 Inf.Bde. will arrange to police the tunnel as far as is necessary.

P.T.O.

7. Pigeons will be sent up to Inf. Bdes. in the line each evening for use the following day; birds if not used should be released two hours before sunset.

8. A Divl. Visual Signal Station will be established in T.4.b. for direct communication to Div. H.Q.

9. Communication with aeroplanes will be carried out as laid down in "Training of Divisions in Offensive Action". Flares will be lit at times ordered or when called for by Contact Patrol aeroplane, which will be marked as follows :-

One black band under the right lower plane with streamers behind the band.

Lieut. Colonel, G.S.,
33rd Division.

21/4/17.

Distribution :-

	Copies.	
Div. H.Q.	5	
Inf. Bdes.	8	each
21 & 37 Div. Arts.	5	each
33 Div. Art.	1	
33 Div. Eng.	1	
18 Middx. R. (Pioneers)	1	
10 Co., D Bn. (H.B) M.G.C.	5	

App Apr 4

Dispositions of 37th D.A.

H.Q. 37th D.A. ... ... HAMELINCOURT. S 29 d 1.8.

123 Brigade R.F.A.   W.Lines.

Brigade Headquarters	... ...	T 7 b 1.1.	
"A" 123	... ...	T 3 b 40.75.	S 6 b 90.20.
"B" 123	... ...	N 33 b 80.20.	S 12 d 60.90.
"C" 123	... ...	N 33 b 30.05.	S 12 d 80.30.
"D" 123	... ...	N 33 b 90.60.	S 11 c 60.40.

124 Brigade R.F.A.

Brigade Headquarters	... ...	N 32 d 30.50.	
"A" 124	... ...	N 34 c 0.3.	T 13 b 4.5.
"B" 124	... ...	N 33 b 0.2.	T 13 c 4.8.
"C" 124	... ...	N 33 a 8.5.	T 13 a 3.1.
"D" 124	... ...	T 3 b 4.6.	S 18 d 7.1.

37th D. A. C.

Headquarters	... ...	S 14 d 4.3.
1)) Sections 2)	... ...	S 20 b 60.70.

21.4.17.

Lieut,
for Bde.Major, 37th Divl.Artillery.

No R37
Vol 22

Hoyt

SECRET

37th Division. "Q".

    I forward herewith the War Diary of the Headquarters, 37th Divisional Artillery, for the month of May. 1917.

2-6-17.

Lieut.
for C. R. A.
37th Divisional Artillery.

WAR DIARY
or
INTELLIGENCE SUMMARY
(Erase heading not required.)

Army Form C. 2118.

Place	Date	Hour	Summary of Events and Information	Remarks and references to Appendices
1917				Map used for reference in this diary. ETERPIGNY Special sheet 51B, NW, NE, SW, SE.
May	1	4 am to 4.8 am	Barrage was fired by us in conjunction with all divisions in VII Corps. heavy officer reporting on effect wind following. Before 4 am there was a steady shelling with 5.9 cm along HINDENBURG line & back area. When our barrage opened this ceased but a number of 4.2 cm air bursts fell on + behind HINDENBURG Front + support line, which we held north of river Sensée. The enemy opened his defensive barrage at 4.3 am at 4.20 am it was heaviest, slackening at 4.20 am and stopped at 4.30 am. He fired 5.9 + 4.2 cm on our front and support and shelled our back country with 77 mm.	App. M/O.R. App. M/2 App./M/3 App/M/4
		3.	The Divisional Artillery supported our general attack by 3rd Army. Zero hour 3.30 am. Operation orders giving barrage etc in appendix, also Appendix Reports giving copy of all intelligence as to progress of the Battle. The enemy appears to be fighting stiffer and holding his strong points more tenaciously than at the ARRAS offensive. He apparently withdraws his guns on 1st & 2nd making our counter battery work more difficult and necessarily less definite. As will be seen from Appendix he is using his machine guns to the greatest advantage, placing them in well chosen natural positions, and extends strong emplacements. Tanks have proved useful in this battle the folding ground appears to be more suitable to them. the trees giving more protection from enemy artillery observers.	
	3/4		Hill D/123 moved to old position N33d 8.5. owing to hostile shelling.	

WAR DIARY / INTELLIGENCE SUMMARY

Army Form C. 2118.

Place	Date	Hour	Summary of Events and Information	Remarks and references to Appendices
1917 May	5+6		Bombardments day & night carried out as ordered. Infantry patrols and clear ground fought	App/M/5
			over on 1st.	
	7		British prisoner came in – He had been wounded when taken and kept with 4 Australians	
			wounded, in a cage in FONTAINE WOOD for 48 hours without food or water, the pit prisoners	
			had been marched to the rear earlier. During our bombardment of the wood the guards and those	
			engaged in fatiguing it fled to the dugouts in N.E. edge thereof. After the first burst of our fire, a	
			German officer came up with a new guard, shell three of the old on the spot. He put the new guard	
			filed and one of our shell blew a hole in the wire of the cage. All escaped and —— the one man	
			from above is taken got in early evening.	
			Bombardment arranged to stop 3 min & then open again at 2 intervals a gun a minute for 2 minutes	
			on NE edge of Wood.	
	8		Usual bombardment of points etc during day. Two bursts at 9.45 p.m. and 11.45 p.m. of wood	
			Barrage of gas shell were put up in front of dugouts while wood was vigorously bombarded by 18 pdr	
			and howzrs.	
	9		A/129 moved to	
	10		A/129 moved out to the wagon lines, B/123 moved out of action to wagon lines.	
	11		Enemy shelled —— during night resulting casualties were 4 O.R. Killed 8 O R	
			wounded 10 horses killed or —— through wounds.	

2449 Wt. W14957/M90 750,000 1/16 J.B.C. & A. Forms/C.2118/12.

Army Form C. 2118.

WAR DIARY
or
INTELLIGENCE SUMMARY

(Erase heading not required.)

Command of

Place	Date	Hour	Summary of Events and Information	Remarks and references to Appendices
1917 May	12		C.R.A. 37th took over line at 10.a.m 12th inst. 33rd Division (less Arty) taking App/M/6 over line from 21 Div. (less Arty) Artillery still in line 37th, 21st, 150 Army Field Arty. Bde. New zones allotted see Opp.	
	12		Enemy appeared known at 9.a.m sending up numerous flares. He again shelled back areas with 21 cm howitzer which however stopped firing when a pre-arranged retaliation was brought off. 10 minutes intense fire on Quarry U.33.a 8.9. (supposed Hdqrs) in conjunction with Heavy Artillery.	
	13		Enemy was quieter. He bombed practically all his shelling to back country; and put over a fair quantity of Shell gas and various calibres. Retaliation of 18 Pdr + 4.5 how was again successful at 12.30 a.m. 21cm howitzers movement was noticed behind Sherripy Ridge and working parties were dispersed. Many enemy been sniped at. He has shewn more care lately and movement + transport often never at the gallop where seen and men often double before being fired at.	
	15		Enemy reported by prisoners to be on the point of retiring to DROCOURT QUEANT LINE. Operation App 7 orders issued straight up attack at short notice. 70 and 29 & 3 Army Field Artillery Bde attached to C.R.A 37th Div night of 15/16th N.W.of CROISILLES.	— 48
	16		Further orders cause to dispute attack ordered for 17th cancelled but	— 9
			Hope same operation to take place at a later date.	
	18		33rd Div Arty. took over command of Artillery in line. 37 C.R.A still to command 37 D.A. as Group.	App/10

2449 Wt. W14957/Mgo 750,000 1/16 J.B.C. & A. Forms/C.2118/12.

WAR DIARY or INTELLIGENCE SUMMARY

Army Form C. 2118.

Place	Date	Hour	Summary of Events and Information	Remarks and references to Appendices
May 1917	18		Enemy artillery has been very much quieter on the front last 3 days. 150 mm A.F. Hode dump shrapnel under 37 D.A. for purposes of attack. Lt Hawkins wounded by premature.	App/M/11
	20		Annual attack on HINDENBURG. Capt Roberts slightly wounded, remained at duty. Capt Leg. C.R.A 37 handed over to C.R.A 33rd Div. 2.15pm Attack of HINDENBURG. Support at 7.15p	App/M/0.R.2
	21		37th D.A. HQ. less Staff Captain, moved to ARRAS.	
	22		37th Division taken over line from River COJEUL T.8.9 MONCHY LE PREUX, 29th Div. Map Reference on Right up to River SCARPE, 37th + 29th comprised VIth Corps. 37th Div H.Q. at in ARRAS taken from C.R.A 37th took over command of all artillery on Div Front. from C.R.A 56th VIS EN ARTOIS Composition of Artillery 37th Div under C.R.A.37 was 3rd D.A 40th + 42nd Bdes and 15th D.A. 70th + 71st Bdes. 12th D.A. took over front of 15th D.A. 12 midday.	SIBSW2.
	23		Much 'strafing' of communications, tracks, roads etc. Air photos show line of shell holes having been organised in front of enemy's line, these also receive special attention.	
	25		One heavy + 2 medium Trench mortars put into line.	
	26		Enemy shelling of back areas become habit - up to recently scattered fire has nt generally been his custom.	
	28		Supporting 29th Div. we are to consolidate + crossroads in O8cII. Bulk. to support 29th Div. + own take med. enterprise.	App M/12
	29		Objectives all gained but by 1am all were back in own front line. Barrage kept up to 8.45am	

Army Form C. 2118.

WAR DIARY
or
INTELLIGENCE SUMMARY

(Erase heading not required.)

Instructions regarding War Diaries and Intelligence Summaries are contained in F. S. Regs., Part II. and the Staff Manual respectively. Title Pages will be prepared in manuscript.

Place	Date	Hour	Summary of Events and Information	Remarks and references to Appendices
May 1917	30		Enemy shell battery position in N5c. Special shipping of area and all ammunition received extra amount of ammunition owing to a suspected relief of enemy.	

Atkinson, MRA

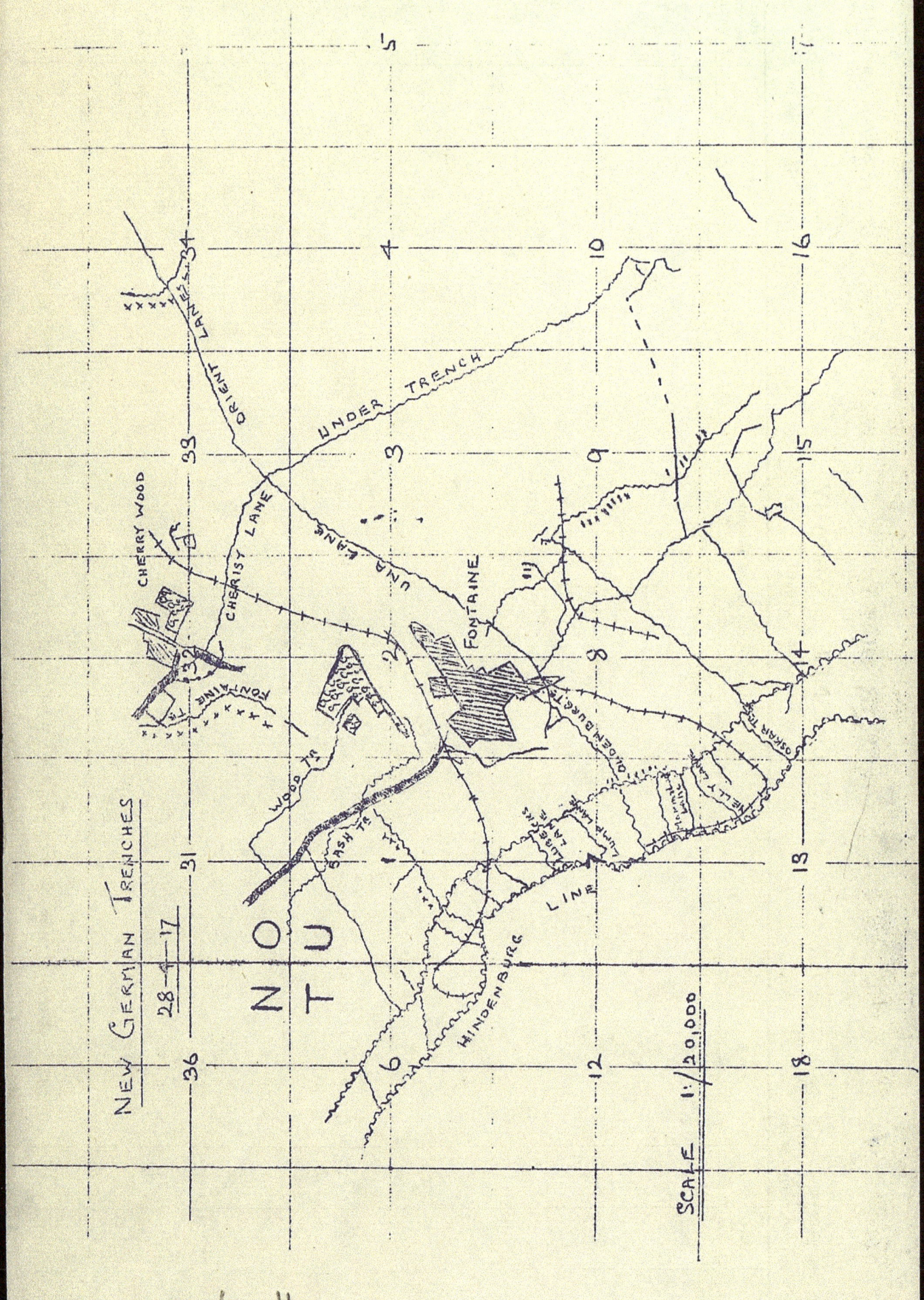

App. W/O R

Page 13.

OPERATION REPORTS.

Date.	Time.		From.	Report.	Action.
	No.	Recd.			
May/17 1st	G.Y/159	5.12 pm	Bde 123.	Before 4 am there was steady shelling by enemy with 5.9's along HINDENBURG and back area. When our barrage opened this ceased and a number of 4.2cm air bursts came on and behind this trench. In front area when our fire opened several thrown red rockets were sent up, but no golden rain. Very heavy barrage opened on our front line at 4.5 am and continued with gradual slackening to 4.30 am. Barrage to North appeared to be still heavier. From 9 am to 10 am Minenwerfer in U2a fired on Uc	

Page I

OPERATION REPORTS.

May 3rd '17.

Date.	Time. No.	Recd.	From.	Report.	Action.
3.5.17	M547	4:29am 4:20am	124	Considerable rifle fire on the left of our zone up to 3:45am. Infantry have left trenches. Red rockets sent up all along the line immediately barrage started. Very few rockets were sent up from FONTAINE – after the first minute nothing.	
	F360	4:41am	124	F.O.O. reports at 4:30am enemy's barrage not very heavy.	
	CB173	4:54am 4:47am	123	Very heavy hostile barrage opened almost simultaneously with ours and heavy machine gun fire from YORK trench and H.G. & rifle fire erased by 4:35am & crft from Hindenburg Trench.	
	CB174	5:1am 4:40am	123	Liaison officer reports 6.4 Inf Bde held up by wire in support trench and steam M.G. fire still coming from CHERRY WOOD.	
	CB175	5:20am 5:10am	123	4:45am some prisoners coming in on our left who all seem to have gone back and a terrific M.G. fire in Hindenburg trench.	
	F361	5:24am 5:32am	124	Barrage timed 5:20am aa C124 F.O.O. cannot see anything but can hear a lot of M.G. fire in the direction of FONTAINE.	
	F367	5:31am	124	Battn liaison officer reports aaa wounded men coming in report heavy M.G. fire from the village of FONTAINE.	

OPERATION REPORTS.

Page 2.

Date.	Time Recd.	No.	From.	Report.	Action.
3.6.17	5.45am 5.30am	GB176	123.	Tank broken down in front of 110" aaa the crew have returned aaa Tank with 6" still working aaa but still held up by wire just beyond starting point.	
	5.55am 5.50am	M648	124	Liaison officer with right Batt. reports aaa hounds all agree that attack was not very strongly aaa he entered the German front line and believe we are now in YORK Trench.	Passed to G.S.O. I.A.
	Verbal Liaison officer 6.19am			aaa infantry are reported just the other side (S.E.) of YORK Trench and are held up there.	
	Verbal 6.15am		125.	Left of Right Batt. is reported at the cross roads V.I.d.7.9. position of right unknown - no news of left Batt. A heavy rifle & m.g. fire is reported to be coming from direction of FONTAINE WOOD.	Passed to G.S.O.I.A. 6.33 am.
	F364 6.34am 6.3am		124	Observing officer reports 6.15am enemy M.G. and rifle fire from the direction of FONTAINE.	
	6.48am 6.40am	M549	124	Batt. Liaison officer reports left of right Batt. is at V.I.d.7.9 aaa no news received of left Batt.	
	Verbal 7.20am		123.	Reported that by Batt. was completely held up, left of left Batt. was reported to be closed to FONTAINE WOOD	

Page 3.

OPERATION REPORTS.

Date.	Time. No.	Recd.	From.	Report.	Action.
3 May/17		7.26am	C.R.A. 21 D.A.	Standing Barrage 300 yards beyond Sensée River as at Z+51-Z+72m but not to its left flank buttress c/o 123. Rate of fire one round per gun per minute line to commence at once	7.30 to 12 Đ 7.31 to 12·y
	Verbal	8·0 am	123 Bde	On left Battn. Bold Rim right on crossroads U16 central and then left N.E corner of wood U2a. They are held up by machine gun fire from U1B 8.2 about and wood.	
	—	8.0 am	12A.	On F.O.O. reports I am with 6th Leicester in U1a. Battalion is unable to move forward until HINDENBURG Support has been taken N of river side. 6th Leicesters are digging in though U1C but are not in touch with Battn. on their right yet, who have been reported held up.	Report asked for — F.O.O. memo 6 Lr. 13th H.Q. avilla.
	—	8.10 a.m.	C.R.A. 21 D.A.	It is reported that our left have got on, bombing is going on in wood. The Division on our left is reported to have captured the blue line.	
	—	8.50 am	21 D.A	123 Bden B/battery to commence firing on same line as the remaining batteries.	123 Bde ordered but given which line, special
	—	8.55 am	21 D.A.	Asked on which line B 123 was to fire on.	"UNA LANE, or main barrage
	—	8.57 am	123.	B 123 is to fire on the main barrage line not on UNA LANE.	line.
	M.S.S.4 9.0 am	9.1 am	124.	Bde Liaison officer reports at 6.50 am we have advanced about 300 yds on existing front line but practically not at all on support line. Fighting in both trenches very hard. Our casualties severe. Our infantry	

OPERATION REPORTS.

Page 4.

Date.	Time Recd.	No.	From.	Report.	Action.
3.5.17	Verbal 9.15 am	Verbal	21.J.A.	digging in along road U.1.d.8.9 to N.W. corner of FONTAINE wood. We have bivouacked wood and fighting. There is progressing in our favour.	refer to 21 J.A. 9.10 am.
	9.19 am	OC124		Halve rate of fire of standing barrage.	passed to 123 F.A.
	10.45 am		124	Juries hit on one gun of B124.	
				Bde Liaison Officer reports, We Pklt tend from U.2.a.0.5. to U.1.b.7.2. Rotten Row as far south as cross roads U.1.d.8.9. thence along sunken road to U.1.d.2.5. north. Am wounded sergeant of 54 inf Bde reports he was wounded E. of Cherisy. There was a gap of 800 yds on their right	
	11.0 am		124 Bde	they had been counter attacked and were expecting another. F.O.O. in T.10 reports. Masses of infantry seen moving in extended order direction S.W. towards road in U.25.	
	11.40 am		123	Liaison Officer reports Boch is attacking in force through FONTAINE Wood.	21 D.A. have a 18pdr and Hows to deal with wood.
	11.45 am		123	— Enemy attacking in face North of Wood.	123 Bde ordered to barrage 200 yds east of Sunken road 0.32.c.9.0 & Centre of wood
	12 noon		124	Col. suggests bringing his barrage back on to bank running S.W. of FONTAINE Wood. They are ordered to do so immediately, to be west of bank.	

OPERATION REPORTS.

Page 5

Date.	Time.		No.	From.	Report.	Action.
	Recd.					
3.5.17	12.15pm		Phone	123	Bodies of hostile infantry seen in road junction in O.33.c and U.3.a and b. Great deal of movement in U.6.	123 Bde Tld to twatch on left flank. They say on left flank is going to attack same enemy still in sunken road O.32.c. on barrage is satisfactory & range. Rate of fire 1rd per min. per gun.
	12.20pm			21.D.A.	18 Division have retired west of CHERISY.	
	12.25pm		M/560	12A	F.O.O. in T.12.a reports 11.45am rifle fire from bank in U.7.b N.E. He cannot see flashes but is certain from direction of sound. No heavies shooting.	
	12.37		CY/28	124	F.O.O. reports 4 parties of men number in all about 100 on road in U.11 marching towards HENDECOURT.	
	12.35		Missing number	124	F.O.O. reports Ammunition wagons moving on the road through U.6 & U.11. Inf. request U.2.a 8.3 and 9.3 to be stopped	123 Hows turned on.
	12.45					
	12.58			124	F.O.O. reports. At 12.45pm three 6 horse teams and outriders seen hitting up track in U.6.A.	Further request for Heavies.
	1.30.				18 Div are reported back in their original alignment.	21 D.A. informed.
	2.19pm			123	As the Poles are in our hands but northern corner of wood south to U.2.a.5.7. & N+S line down to bank S.E. of wood and to go up to U.2.a 8.8. and teams and limbers seen coming S.W. on road through U.6.6. They leave road at U.11.6.6.9 and 50 to O.4 central.	Barrage requested starting point. 123 Bde to put on barrage.
	2.25pm					
	3.10pm		M/562	12A.	Ammn wagons still pass in both directions on road in U.6. F.O.O. reports at 2.30pm. Found from heavy battery fired at U.6.b.85.30. fixed by our own O.O. and	

OPERATION REPORTS.

Page 6.

Date.	Time. Recd.	No.	From.	Report.	Action.
3.5.17	3.10pm	M/562	124.	(contind) and at time to be arranged. This round fell just in front of a wagon causing much confusion and apparent indecision. Wagons finally left at a gallop going towards CAGNICOURT. No further rounds from our heavies were fired. Several other wagons arrived soon afterwards leaving road at U11b2.4. Making to U4central. All wagons previous to this left road U11b6.9. Suggest any S.O.S. heavies having O.P. overlooking this zone be informed no single round has caused traffic to stop.	123 have already been told to get their into touch with a battery.
	4.56pm	G879	123	Motor Buses and Transport still using road through U6b & HENDECOURT.	Heavies again asked to fire.
	6.30pm		21 D.A. + Divn. A.	Attack to take place 7.15 down Wood Trench, Rest, FONTAINE WOOD along river. Barrage to be arranged by 37 D.A. 7.15 to 7.25 3 rds per gun per min. 18 pdr 3 rds per ton per min. 7.25 to 7.35 one round per gun per min. Barrage Eastern + Southern edge of wood.	6.35 passed to 123 6.40 — ·124.
	7.34/u to 42B/A			C.R.A. 37 D.A. proposes to continue barrage on same line at half a round per gun per min. until infantry are satisfied.	7.34/u passed to 1/24
	7.40/u	F398	124	F.O.O. reports at 7.29pm enemy putting up heavy barrage on our left.	7.50/u passed to 21/1.A.
	9.29pm	Verbal to 123 & 124		Increase rate of fire on present barrage lines to 2rds per gun per minute. Enemy counter attacking on WOOD TRENCH (Right Battn. 110 Bde) report from division officer Right Bde.	
	Phone 8.38pm		Liaison Officer Infantry Brigadier is quite satisfied with 7.15 counter attack + thinks barrage can be reduced.		123 to reduce barrage 124 to 1 round per gun per minute.

OPERATION REPORTS.

Page 7.

Date.	Time. Recd.	No.	From.	Report.	Action.
3.5.17	9.45pm	Verbal	Liaison Officer 110 Bde	Enemy counter attack has driven our left Bn out of woods TRENCH, and a heavy barrage is now on E of Brown line. Right Bn 15/D.L.I. and Rt. Bn. B.C. are where they were before, the latter along the sunken road. U.1.d.7.9 & thence westwards.	passed to 2nd I.A.
	9.58pm	Verbal	A.S.	Night tasks (when counter-attack has ceased) will be (1) Edge of wood U.2.a.7-6 to U.2.b.15-20 (2) Sand Road U.2.b.9.5-6.0 to U.2.d.2-7 Rate of fire 6 salvoes per battery per hour.	
	10pm	Verbal	12u	Night task (when situation is suitable) will be 15/Drs on Riverbed 0.3.2.d.7-0 to U.2.c.0-6 15eet/Drs on Bridge U.2.c.10.5.5 18/Drs on Sa woco per battery per hour. Rates of fire 30 rounds per hour.	
	10.40pm	Liaison Officer		We are all back on an original line of this morning. same as last night	
	10.45	Liaison Offr		Liaison Officer says present barrage to stop get onto S.O.S lines and remain without firing, ready.	123} Bdes told 124}

OPERATION REPORTS.

Page 8

Date.	Time Recd.	No.	From.	Report.	Action.
4.5.17.	7.10pm		123.	Night fairly quiet since 10.30 pm. Liaison Officer reports some of our men still holding out in YORK TRENCH & requests that the heavies Artillery should be informed.	Liaison Officer already told Bdes not to fire to a home.
	8.30am	MT/786	110th & Bde	It is intended to withdraw the infantry that remain in' YORK TRENCH this morning, please inform all batteries covering the front.	
	5.35 pm	G1	124. y	Liaison Officer Prince (110th Bde) reports Prince holds trench from T6D 50.95 to U1A 30.50 but remainder of this trench is clear of enemy. Bush Trench is also clear to about U1B.S.A. York Trench is manned by enemy. Wood Trench is only from 1 to 2 feet deep. Salvage will be carried out in U1A around BUSH TRENCH and as soon as possible to YORK TRENCH so that until 3 A.M. a good margin of fire should be allowed. S.O.S lines should not be fired on unless absolutely necessary.	
	8.55pm	13/log	123 Bde	Liaison Officer wires. Wiring Party will be out 40 yards in front of 'Blue' T6 b 12. & O 31 a 9.0. all night.	
	9.50 pm	BM/207	21.D.A.	Patrols will be out reconnoitring YORK TRENCH from 2 am to 3 a.m. Arrange accordingly.	
	7.43am	F/163	124	F.O.O. reports movement still visible in U6 and U11.	
	2.37am	B/45		Liaison Officer reports 6 inch 60 pdr firing short in O 31.C 4.6.	
	10.30 am	Phone	Liaison Officer	New S.O.S lines as follows are required. U1C 55.65 U1C 30.90 U1B 45.45. O 31d 0.0. O 31 b 20.10. U1C 35.10 O 31C 4.6.	

OPERATION REPORTS.

Page 9

Date.	Time. Recd.	No.	From.	Report.	Action.
5.5.17	10.45a	9/5	Liaison Officer	Brown line held by Northumberland Fusiliers 13 Battalion, 1 Company of 12th N.F. are in element of Trench T6 b 12 to T6 b 50.58. and half in Trench running from T6 d 5.9 as reported before. This Trench is emergency bypassway before a cable trench at T6 b 50.58.	
	12.20p		Phone 21.D.A.	BUSH Trench is occupied by enemy up to U1 b 35.50 There are still a number of our men lying out in shell holes in front of YORK Trench and infantry are going to get them in this morning. There are said to be no enemy North of U1 b 35.50.	Boles told to keep their tie 2nd 2 Runs until Liaison Officer reports safe.

Ref.Map.　　　　37th Divisional Artillery Operation　　　23
51 b S.W.　　　SECRET　　Order No:55.　　Opp. M/1
1/20,000

　　　　　　　Reference 21st Div.Arty.Operation Order No:57, dated
　　　　1st May,1917:-
1.　　Para 5 (b) D/123 Bde.R.F.A. & D/124 Bde.R.F.A. to carry out this
　　　task from Z-5 to Z-3 firing B.C.B.R. at rate of 100 rounds
　　　per battery per hour.
　　　Para 5 (c) It has been arranged for 94th Bde.R.F.A. to engage
　　　Trench Junction U 1 C 4.5 . . . . and portion of trench
　　　U 1 C 4.5 - U 1 C 7.6. 37th Div.Arty.tasks will therefore
　　　remain as at present.

2.　　　　　Para.8. "Creeping barrage".(a) -(vide attached
　　　diagram)

　　　Zero to　　　　124 Bde. .. N 36 D 80.00 - O 31 C 50.50
　　　Zero plus 2　　123 Bde. .. O 31 C 50.50 - O 31 B 20.10

　　　Zero plus
　　　20 to Zero　　 124 Bde. .. U 1 D 70.90 - U 2 A 30.50
　　　plus 24　　　　123 Bde. .. U 2 A 30.50 - U 32 C 70.10

　　　Zero plus
　　　51 to Zero　　 124 Bde. .. U 2 C 20.30 - U 2 D 10.80
　　　plus 2 hours.　123 Bde. .. U 2 D 10.80 - U 3 A 20.10

　　　Zero plus 2
　　　hrs.54 to zero 124 Bde. .. U 8 D 00.90 - U 3 C 45.00
　　　plus 3 hours.　123 Bde. .. U 3 C 45.00 - U 4 C 00.30

3.　　　　　From zero plus 2 hours the battery on the left of
　　　37th Divisional Artillery barrage (B/123) will conform with
　　　rate of movement of division on Left flank, moving at rate
　　　of 100 yards in 3 minutes until reaching line U 3 C 45.00 -
　　　U 4 C 00.30 where it will remain until zero plus 3 hours,
　　　ceasing fire with the remainder.

4.　　　　　Para.8 (b). D/123 Trench O 31 C 80.20 - U 2 A 30.50
　　　　　　　　　　　　 D/124 Road   O 31 C 60.40 - U 2 C 10.60
　　　On moving off with Creeping Barrage at Zero plus 2 hours
　　　both batteries will work through FONTAINE village at rate
　　　laid down, ceasing fire on reaching Eastern outskirts of vil-
　　　lage at zero plus 2 hours 24 mins.

5.　　　　　Watches will be synchronised at hours stated
　　　direct with 21st Div.Arty.Headquarters.

6.　　　　　Para.14. Infantry Brigade Liaison Officer will move
　　　to 110th Infantry Brigade H.Qrs. at 10 a.m. 2nd instant.

7.　　　　　Acknowledge.

Issued at 1 am.
2nd May/17.　　　　　　　　　　　　　　　　　　Major
　　　　　　　　　　　　　　　Brigade Major,37th Divl.Artillery.

　　　　Copies to:-　21st Div.　No:1　　123 Bde.R.F.A.　6 - 10
　　　　　　　　　　　21st D.A.　　 2　　124 Bde.R.F.A.　11 - 15
　　　　　　　　　　　18th D.A.　　 3　　Liaison Officer　16
　　　　　　　　　　　110 Inf.Bde.　4　　37th D.A.C.　　　17
　　　　　　　　　　　94th Bde.R.F.A. 5　Staff Capt.　　　18
　　　　　　　　　　　　　　　　　Sig.Officer 19
　　　　　　　　　　　　　　　　　Staff Capt. 20
　　　　　　　　　　　　　　　　　Office　 21 & 22
　　　　　　　　　　　　　　　　　Diary　　23 & 24

Ref.Map.
51 b S.W.
1/20,000

37th Divisional Artillery Operation Order No:55.

SECRET

24

Reference 21st Div.Arty.Operation Order No:57, dated 1st May,1917:-

1. Para 5 (b) D/123 Bde.R.F.A. & D/124 Bde.R.F.A. to carry out this task from Z- 5 to Z- 3 firing B.C.B.R. at rate of 100 rounds per battery per hour.
Para 5 (c) It has been arranged for 94th Bde.R.F.A. to engage Trench Junction U 1 C 4.5   and portion of trench U 1 C 4.5 - U 1 C 7.6. 37th Div.Arty.tasks will therefore remain as at present.

2. Para.8. "Creeping barrage".(a) -(vide attached diagram)

Zero to Zero plus 2	124 Bde.	N 36 D 80.00	- O 31 C 50.50
	123 Bde.	O 31 C 50.50	- O 31 B 20.10
Zero plus 20 to Zero plus 24	124 Bde.	U 1 D 70.90	- U 2 A 30.50
	123 Bde.	U 2 A 30.50	- U 32 C 70.10
Zero plus 51 to Zero plus 2 hours.	124 Bde.	U 2 C 20.30	- U 2 D 10.80
	123 Bde.	U 2 D 10.80	- U 3 A 20.10
Zero plus 2 hrs.54 to zero plus 3 hours.	124 Bde.	U 2 D 00.90	- U 3 C 45.00
	123 Bde.	U 3 C 45.00	- U 4 C 00.30

3. From zero plus 2 hours the battery on the left of 37th Divisional Artillery barrage (B/123) will conform with rate of movement of division on Left flank, moving at rate of 100 yards in 3 minutes until reaching line U 3 C 45.00 - U 4 C 00.30 where it will remain until zero plus 3 hours, ceasing fire with the remainder.

4. Para.8 (b). D/123 Trench O 31 C 80.20 - U 2 A 30.50
D/124 Road O 31 C 60.40 - U 2 C 10.60
On moving off with Creeping Barrage at Zero plus 2 hours both batteries will work through FONTAINE village at rate laid down, ceasing fire on reaching Eastern outskirts of village at zero plus 2 hours 24 mins.

5. Watches will be synchronised at hours stated direct with 21st Div.Arty.Headquarters.

6. Para.14. Infantry Brigade Liaison Officer will move to 110th Infantry Brigade H.Qrs. at 10 a.m. 2nd instant.

7. Acknowledge.

Issued at 1 am.
2nd May/17.

Major
Brigade Major, 37th Divl.Artillery.

Copies to:- 21st Div.   No:1   123 Bde.R.F.A. 6 - 10
             21st D.A.   2   124 Bde.R.F.A. 11 - 15
             18th D.A.   3   Liaison Officer   16
             110 Inf.Bde.   4   37th D.A.C.   17
             94th Bde.R.F.A.   5   Staff Capt.   18
                                    Sig.Officer   19
                                    Staff Capt.   20
                                    Office   21 & 22
                                    Diary   23 & 24

S E C R E T.   C/153/12.

Reference 37th D.A.O.O. No.55 dated 2.5.17, para. 3 :-

the time now for left flank battery (B.123) to cease fire, will be Zero plus 2 hours 30 minutes NOT Zero plus 3 hours.

This is in accordance with addendum to 21 D.A.O.O. No.57, attached, para.1.

                                                                         Major,

2.5.17.   Bde. Major,   37th Div. Arty.

To 37th D.A
For information
M Shea[?]
2.5.17

App/M/3[?]

HEADQUARTERS.
21st
DIVISIONAL ARTILLERY.
No. BM 231

SECRET.

VII Corps G.C.R. 604/452.

14th Division.
18th Division.
21st Division.
33rd Division.
50th Division.
G.O.C., R.A.
VII Corps Heavy Artillery.
No. 8 Squadron, R.F.C.
3rd Balloon Wing, R.F.C.
Vth Corps.
VIth Corps.
1st Brigade H.B., M.G.C.
VII Corps "Q".
Chemical Adviser.
File.

    At Zero a concentrated bombardment will commence with Chemical Shell, as per Table attached, and will last until Zero plus 30 minutes.

    If the weather conditions are unsuitable for the use of Chemical Shell, H.E. will be used.

    ACKNOWLEDGE.

1st May, 1917.

George Crossman Major
for
Brigadier-General,
General Staff, VII Corps.

VII CORPS HEAVY ARTILLERY.

Targets :-   PA.2.,   PC.2.,   PC.3.

Zero to plus 3 mins.   65 rounds C.B.R. on each target.) Total.
3 mins. to   27 mins. 120   "   P.S.   "   "   "   ) C.B.R. 390.
27 mins. to 30 mins. 65   "   C.B.R. "   "   "   ) P.S.   360.

Sufficient batteries to be detailed to allow of rate of fire being normal.

14th DIVISIONAL ARTILLERY.

Targets :-   OD.14.,   OD.17.

Zero to plus 3 mins.   80 rounds C.B.R. on each target.) Total.
3 mins. to   27 mins. 60   "   S.K.   "   "   "   ) C.B.R. 320.
27 mins. to 30 mins. 80   "   C.B.R. "   "   "   ) S.K.   120.

18th DIVISIONAL ARTILLERY.

Targets :-   OD.6.,   OD.12.

Zero to plus 3 mins.   80 rounds C.B.R. on each target.) Total.
3 mins. to   27 mins. 60   "   S.K.   "   "   "   ) C.B.R. 320.
27 mins. to 30 mins. 80   "   C.B.R. "   "   "   ) S.K.   120.

****

No 2/27   Date 2.5.17.

O.C.   123 Bde. R.F.A.
       124 Bde. R.F.A.

Ref. 37th D.A.O.O. 55 of 2.5.17.
para 1. The Lethal shell bombardment
will not commence without
definite instructions to that
effect from this office.

Acknowledge.

                              Ranimbai

No L/28.　　　　　　　　　　　　　　　　　SECRET.
　　　　　　　　　　　DATE 2.V.17.
O.C. 123rd Bde R.F.A.
　　　124th Bde R.F.A.　　　　| Ref. 51b S.W. 1/20000 |

Ref. 21st D.A.O.D. No 57 - para 5(a) - "Bombardment of
FONTAINE Wood with Lethal Shell" night Y/Z.

① Tasks. D/123.
　　　　　edge of wood. U2a50.68 - U2a40.50.
　　　　　edge of spinney. U2a39.45 - U2a29.38.

　　D/124.
　　　　　U2a74.50 - U2a79.20.

② Each task should receive 300 rounds per hour
per battery, equally distributed.
　　As there is only sufficient ammunition
for one hour, the shoot will take place
from Zero-4 to Zero-3 on receipt of definite
orders from this office.

③ Any ammunition over and above the 300
rounds which may be in hand, should be
fired at the same rate of fire, fire being
opened in sufficient time before Zero-4
to allow of the extra expenditure.
　　Firing must be continuous throughout
the whole period and no lethal shell

Must be fried after Zero-3.

Acknowledge.

C.R.A.   App/M/3   COPY NO. 1

21ST DIVISIONAL ARTILLERY OPERATION ORDER NO. 57.

Ref. Map.1/20,000   1st May 1917.
Sheet 51b.SW.

1. The Third Army is continuing the attack on 3rd May 1917.

   The V Corps are attacking simultaneously on our Right.

2. The objectives of the 21st Division are as follows :-

   (a) The BLUE Line ... ... Line of the SENSEE River.
   (b) The YELLOW Line ... ... T.18.b.5.3. - U.7.c.0.0. - U.7.c.5.5.
       - U.7.d.1.5. - U.7.d.7.7. - U.8.c.0.8
       - U.8.a.5.4. - U.8.b.0.7. - U.2.d.4.0
       - U.2.d.6.4.

3. The advance of the 21st Division will be carried out as follows:

   (a) The BLUE and YELLOW Line S.W. of the HINDENBURG Front Trench (exclusive) by the 62nd Inf. Bde.
       Neither of these advances will be made until further orders are received from Divisional Headquarters.

   (b) South-eastwards along HINDENBURG Line (Front and Support Trenches inclusive) to the Army Boundary, by the 64th Inf. Bde.

   (c) To the BLUE and YELLOW Lines N.E. of the HINDENBURG Support Line (exclusive) by the 110th Inf. Bde.

4. Prior to the attack, 110th Inf. Bde. will take over from 64th Inf. Bde. all positions North and North-east of HINDENBURG Support Trench now held by latter Brigade.

   110th Inf. Bde. will also take over 500 yards of Front from the Right Brigade of 18th Division.

5. BOMBARDMENT.

   The Bombardment at present in progress will continue until Zero hour on 'Z' Day (May 3rd).   There must be no cessation of fire immediately before Zero.

   On Y/Z Night, FONTAINE WOOD will be bombarded with Lethal Shell by 37th Div.Art. and 95th Bde R.F.A. (Wind Permitting) up till 3 hours before Zero.   B.C.B.R. Ammunition now in possession of above units will be used.

2.

5. Contd.

The Trench Junction U.1.c.4.5. and Trench U.1.c.4.5. to U.1.b.8.2. will be bombarded during Y/Z Night by 37th Div. Art. and 94th Bde R.F.A.

At 2 hours before Zero, FONTAINE Wood will be bombarded with Incendiary Shell (weather permitting) by 94th Bde R.F.A. Thermit Shells have been issued today for this purpose. They must be stored separately from other shells.

6. On 'Z' Day, all Echelons will be full.

7. On 'Z' Day, the 95th Bde R.F.A. will be harnessed up ready to move at short notice.

8. CREEPING BARRAGE.

    (a) 37th Div. Art.   6-18pdr Batteries.

         94th Bde R.F.A.   2-18pdr Batteries.(C/94 & A/94)

    The Creeping Barrage to be kept 200 yards clear of HINDENBURG Support Trench.

    At Zero, the Creeping Barrage will open with a Salvo from all Batteries, on the Line T.6.b.2.7. - N.36.d.8.0. - O.31.c.5.5. - O.31.b.2.1.

    94th Bde RFA.   T.6.b.2.7. - N.36.d.8.0.

    37th Div.Art.   N.36.d.8.0. - O.31.b.2.1.

    At 2 minutes after Zero, it will creep forward at the rate of 100 yards in 2 minutes, until it reaches the Line of the Road U.1.d.1.4. - U.1.d.7.9. - O.32.c.7.1.

    94th Bde RFA.   U.1.d.1.4. - U.1.d.7.8.

    37th Div.Art.   U.1.d.7.8. - O.32.c.7.1.

    At 24 minutes after Zero, it will creep forward at the rate of 100 yards in 6 minutes, until it reaches the a line about 200 yards beyond the SENSEE River, i.e., U.7.b.7.7. - U.2.c.2.3. - U.2.d.0.7. - U.2.b.5.0. - U.2.b.1.1.

    94th Bde RFA.   U.7.b.7.7. - U.2.c.2.3.

    37th Div.Art.   U.2.c.2.3. - U.2.b.1.1.

    It will remain on this Line until 2 hours after Zero.

                                                At 2 hours

8. Contd.

> At 2 hours after Zero, it will creep forward at the rate of 100 yards in 6 minutes, until it reaches the Line U.8.c.3.3. - U.8.d.0.9. - U.9.a.0.8. - U.3.a.5.0 - U.3.d.0.1. - U.4.c.0.3.
>
> 94th Bde RFA.   U.8.c.3.3. - U.8.d.0.9.
>
> 37th Div.Art.   U.8.d.0.9. - U.4.c.0.3.
>
> At 3 hours after Zero, it will cease.

(b)   The Two 4.5 Howitzer Batteries of 37th Div. Art. will barrage the German Trenches O.31.c.8.2. to U.2.a.3.5., and Road O.31.c.6.4. to U.2.c.1.6.

> At Zero, these Two Batteries will conform with the Creeping Barrage, and creep down the Trenches and Road through FONTAINE Village and Wood in conjunction with Creeping Barrage (a)

9. **STANDING BARRAGE & SPECIAL TASKS.**

(a)   1-18pdr Battery   94th Bde RFA.   (B/94)

   1-4.5 How. Battery   94th Bde RFA.   (D/94)

> At Zero, these Batteries will form a Standing Barrage on the edge of FONTAINE Wood U.2.a.5.0. to U.2.a.3.3. and Road U.2.a.3.3. to U.2.a.5.7.
>
> At 24 minutes after Zero, when the Creeping Barrage moves off Road U.2.a.3.3. to U.2.a.5.7., this Standing Barrage will conform with the Creeping Barrage, and creep through the Wood at the rate of 100 yards in 6 minutes, to a Line 200 yards beyond the SENSEE River.
>
> At 48 minutes after Zero, this Standing Barrage will cease.
>
> These two Batteries will then come under the immediate orders of the Brig-General Comdg. 110th Inf. Bde. in order that their fire may be again turned on FONTAINE Wood, or on to any hostile position which may be holding up the advance, at short notice if necessary.

(b)   150th AFA Bde

9. Contd.

    (b) <u>150th Army Field Art. Bde.</u>   3-18pdr Batteries.

                                            1-4.5 Howitzer Battery.

       <u>At Zero</u>, the above Batteries will establish an Enfilade Barrage on the German Trench U.1.c.7.7. to U.1.b.8.2. and Road U.1.d.1.4. to U.1.d.8.9. to U.2.a.2.3. to U.2.a.5.7., keeping 200 yards clear of HINDENBURG Support Trench.

       <u>At 18 minutes after Zero</u>, this Barrage will switch off the Trench on to Road U.1.d.1.4. - U.1.d.8.9. - U.2.a.2.3. - U.2.a.5.7.

       <u>At 24 minutes after Zero</u>, it will switch on to a Line 200 yards beyond the SENSEE River, i.e., the Line U.7.a.9.3. - U.7.b.4.5. - U.7.b.8.9. - U.2.c.2.3. - U.2.d.0.7. - U.3.a.0.2.

       It will remain on this Line until 40 minutes after Zero.

       <u>At 40 minutes after Zero</u>, it will switch on to the YELLOW Line, i.e., to the Line U.7.d.1.5. - U.7.d.7.7. - U.8.c.0.8. - U.8.a.5.4. - U.8.b.0.7. - U.2.d.4.0 - U.2.b.9.0.

       <u>At 2 hours after Zero</u>, it will switch on to a Line 300 yards beyond the YELLOW Line, i.e., to the Line U.7.d.3.0. - U.8.c.3.3. - U.8.d.0.9. - U.8.b.7.5. - U.3.c.0.0.

       <u>At 2 hours & 30 minutes after Zero</u>, it will cease.

    (c) <u>95th Brigade R.F.A.</u>   1-18pdr Battery
                                1-4.5 Howitzer Battery.

       <u>At Zero</u>, these Batteries will establish an Enfilade Barrage on the Line of the SENSEE River U.7.a.8.5. to U.7.b.2.7. and on HINDENBURG System from the Line U.7.b.0.0. - U.7.b.5.3. to U.7.a.8.5. - U.7.b.2.7.

       <u>At 15 minutes after Zero</u>, this Barrage will switch on to the Line of the Road U.7.b.0.0. - U.7.b.5.3., to the Line U.7.a.9.2. - U.7.b.5.5., and will thicken up the Heavy Artillery Barrage on this area.

       <u>At 40 minutes after Zero</u>, it will switch on to the YELLOW Line, i.e., the Line U.7.d.1.5. - U.7.d.7.7. - U.8.c.0.8. - U.8.a.5.4.

       It will remain on this Line until 2 hours after Zero.

                                                At 2 hours after

9. Contd.

   (c) Contd.

      At 2 hours after Zero, it will switch on to a Line 300 yards beyond the YELLOW Line, i.e., the Line U.7.d.3.0. - U.8.c.3.3. - U.8.d.0.9. - U.8.b.7.5. - U.3.c.2.2.

      At 2 hours & 30 minutes after Zero, it will cease.

   (d) <u>95th Bde RFA.</u>   2-18pdr Batteries (less 1 Section)

      At Zero, these Batteries will establish an Enfilade Barrage on the YELLOW Line U.7.d.1.5. - U.7.d.7.7. - U.8.c.0.8. - U.8.a.5.4.

      It will remain on this Line until 2 hours after Zero.

      It will then conform with Standing Barrage (c).

   (e) <u>95th Bde RFA.</u>   1 Section A/95.

     The special task of this Section will be to bring Reverse Fire to bear on the German Trench U.1.c.7.7. - U.1.b.8.2. and Road U.1.d.1.4. - U.1.d.8.9. - U.2.a.2.3. - U.2.a.5.7., and the successive objectives of Standing Barrage (b).

     The fire of this Section will conform to the Lifts of Standing Barrage (b) of 150th Army Field Arty. Bde. The lifts off the successive objectives taking place in each case 3 minutes earlier than the lifts laid down for 150th Army Field Arty. Bde.

10. <u>HEAVY ARTILLERY.</u>

   (a) <u>At Zero,</u> the VII Corps Heavy Artillery will bombard the HINDENBURG SYSTEM from the Army Boundary U.14.c.1.9. - U.14.a.6.2. to the Line U.7.a.9.3. - U.7.b.4.5.

   (b) <u>At 40 minutes after Zero,</u> the Heavy Artillery will lift on to the YELLOW Line U.7.d.1.5. - U.7.d.8.8. *small area*

   (c) The Heavy Artillery Barrage will remain on the YELLOW Line U.7.d.1.5. - U.7.d.8.8. until 2 hours after Zero, unless a Signal is given by the WAVING OF FLAGS from the HINDENBURG Trench.

   (d) If flags are waved before <u>2 hours after Zero</u>, it will mean that 64th Inf. Bde. are ready to advance beyond the YELLOW Line. The Heavy Artillery Barrage will then move back to the Line U.7.d.2.0. - U.7.d.9.3.

                                       (e) If No

10 Contd.

    (e) If no flags are waved, the Heavy Artillery Barrage will move back on to the Line U.7.d.2.0. - U.7.d.9.2. at <u>2 hours after Zero.</u>

    (f) The Heavy Artillery Barrage will remain on the Line U.7.d.2.0 - U.7.d.9.2. - U.8.d.0.8. - U.3.c.2.0. until 3½ hours after zero, when it will cease.

11. <u>NOTE for 95th and 150th Bdes R.F.A.</u>

    Standing Barrages (b), (c), and (d) of 95th and 150th Bde R.F.A. will, on arrival at the YELLOW Line, conform to the Heavy Artillery Lifts.
    These Barrages will remain on the YELLOW Line until <u>2 hours after Zero</u>, unless a Signal is given by the WAVING OF FLAGS from the HINDENBURG Trench.

12. <u>RATES OF FIRE.</u>

    <u>Creeping Barrage</u>   <u>18 pounders</u>.

Zero to 20 mins after Zero, ...	3 rds per gun per min
20 mins after Zero to 1 hour after Zero	2 : :
1 hour after Zero to 2 hours after Zero	1 : :
2 hours after Zero to 2hrs 30 mins :	2 : :
2 hours 30 mins after Zero to 3hrs :	1 : :

    <u>4.5 Howitzers.</u>

Zero to 20 mins after Zero	2 rds per how per min.
20 mins after Zero to 2 hrs after Zero	1 : :
2 hrs after Zero to 2hrs 30 mins :	2 : :

    <u>Standing Barrages</u>   <u>18 pounders.</u>

Zero to 50 mins after Zero ...	2 rds per gun per min.
50 mins after Zero to 2hrs 30mins after Zero	1 : :

    <u>4.5 Howitzers.</u>

Zero to 40 mins after Zero	2 rds per how per min
40 mins after Zero to 2hrs 30mins after Zero	1 : :

13. <u>WATCHES.</u>

    Watches will be very carefully synchronised on May 2nd and 3rd.
    On May 2nd at 9.am. and 6.pm. and on May 3rd at 2.30.a.

14. **LIAISON.**

The 37th Div.Art. and 94th Bde RFA. will have Liaison Officers with 110th Inf. Bde.

The 95th Bde RFA. will have a Liaison Officer with 64th Inf. Bde.

The 150th Army Field Arty Bde. will have a Liaison Officer with 62nd Inf. Bde.

M Sinclair Major R.A.
Brigade Major, 21st Divisional Artillery.

Issued at 9.15.pm. to :-

```
        37th Div.Art.      Copies Nos.   1 - 15  (Inc.Liaison Officer)
        94th Bde RFA.          :        16 - 22                :
        95th     :             :        23 - 29                :
        150th    :             :        30 - 36                :
        21st D. A. C.          :        37 - 40
        21 Div 'G'             :        41 - 45
             'Q'               :           46
        R.A. VII Corps         :        47 - 48
        H.A.    :              :           49
         8th H. A. G.          :           50
        46th    :              :           51
        18th Div.Art.          :           52
        32nd    :              :           53
        8th Sq.R.F.C.          :           54
        S.C.R.A. 21 Div.       :           55
        Sig.Offr.  :  Art.     :           56
        War Diary              :        57 - 58
```

SECRET.   APPENDIX 'A'

Ref. 21st Div. Art. O.O. No.57 dated
1/5/1917.
* * * * *

1.   The 21st Division will consolidate and hold FONTAINE LEZ CROISILLES, and will be prepared to assist the 18th Division in case of counter-attack.   If necessity arises 18th Division will call on 21st Division direct.

2. (a)   The Batteries of the 95th Brigade R.F.A. now in action North of CROISILLES will be prepared to move at short notice into the area U.13. and U.19., after the 21st Division has occupied FONTAINE LEZ CROISILLES.   Orders for this move will be issued from 21st Div. Art. H.Qrs.

   (b)   The 150th Army Field Arty. Bde. will reconnoitre positions about T.12.

   (c)   The task of these Brigades will be to support the Right of the 18th Division, and assist that Division in case of counter-attack.
   The general line of fire will be approximately the WOOD in O.35. and U.5.

3.   One 18pdr Battery in each Brigade, the 4.5 Howitzer Battery of 150th Army Field Arty. Bde., and one 4.5 Howitzer Battery of 37th Divnl. Arty. will be detailed to answer calls from the air, and be prepared to take on hostile counter-attacks.

4.   Batteries after moving forward, must wire in their positions.   Assistance will be given by Divisional Pioneers if required.

5.   Four Tanks have been allotted to 21st Division for the operations on May 3rd.

6.   Flares will be lit by leading troops at 1½ hours after Zero, and 3½ hours after Zero, when called for by Contact Aeroplane firing WHITE Very Lights or sounding Klaxon Horn, and at any other time called for by Contact Aeroplane.

7.   Distinguishing Marks.

   (a)   YELLOW Flags with Black Divisional Sign in the Centre are to be used by 64th Inf. Bde.
   These flags have no meaning unless waved, and are only to be used by leading troops.

   (b)   Units of 62nd Division detailed for the third (RED) Objective, are to wear a piece of bright tin 4" square on the back.
   62nd Division are also carrying RED Flags and GREEN Flags.

Para.8 /
PTO

8. Synchronisation of Watches.

   Watches will be synchroised from Div. H.Qrs., at midnight on 2/3rd May.

   Infantry and Artillery Brigades will also carefully compare watches through Liaison Officers.

9.   The Artillery of the VII Corps will not fire South-east of the Line of the Army Boundary. i.e., Line U.14.c.3.9. - U.9.c.0.4. - U.9.b.0.2. - U.4.c.0.0.

2/5/1917.   *J.M.Sinclair* Major R.A.
           Brigade-Major, 21st Divisional Artillery.

   Issued at 6.30.pm. to all recipients of O.O. 57.

www.ingramcontent.com/pod-product-compliance
Lightning Source LLC
Chambersburg PA
CBHW081536160426
43191CB00011B/1771